Gorgeous glimpses into the etern
with the next generation. This bc
children ...and likely you with it!

—Alan Charter
Facilitator for the Global Children's Forum

In my work with youth, I often tell them, "You don't have the change the world," but I go on to say, "Because God is already out there changing it, and you get to be a part of His work." In *Discipling World Changers*, Melissa reminds us of the same thing – we don't have to make our kids follow Jesus, we get to join Christ in the work He is already doing in their hearts. With heartwarming stories, practical applications, real-life experiences, and heartfelt convictions, Melissa invites parents and ministers to discover who we are and rediscover who God is as we work out how we help our children follow us as we follow Christ. This is the kind of book you'll want to take one chapter at a time and marinate in the invitation offered through each chapter and follow-up questions and allow the Spirit to heal old wounds, open new understandings, and produce the fruit of a disciple in your own heart even as you disciple your children.

—Rev. Dr. Christina Embree
Founder/Director of ReFocus Ministry

Some people are good pastors. Others are good speakers. Others are good trainers. Others are good writers.

Rarely do you find someone who is all four. Melissa MacDonald is. And her gifts are on full display in *Discipling World Changers*. As I read her words, I found my mind dominated by two thoughts. First..."I would have been a much better youth pastor had I read this book 30 years ago!" Second..."I would have loved my kids to have been discipled by Melissa."

Discipling World Changers is a rare blend of foundational discipleship philosophy, much-needed encouragement, and practical application. And because Mel is a world-class storyteller, you'll find yourself laughing, crying, and cheering all the way through.

If you have kids or work with kids, this should be the next book you read. The kids you raise and serve will love Jesus more deeply, authentically, and joyfully after you do.

—Keith Ferrin
Author & Speaker (keithferrin.com)

Discipling World Changers is a game-changing book! I'm so blessed to have had the opportunity to read my sister (I think we were separated at birth?) Melissa MacDonald has written.

Her approach to discipling children is powerful and solid from Scripture. Her perspective challenges many because they make discipleship about them when it is about pointing children to Jesus.

"Discipleship continues beyond us; we won't see it all" is such a powerful truth, and if leaders will grab that and realize that it doesn't depend on only them, but it takes parents, small group leaders, friends, pastors, and so many more to build up a child in the faith and sometimes we don't see the end of the process in our lifetime.

I love Mel's focus on being authentic, simple, loving, and modeling who Jesus is so kids understand they can truly know and love him just as they are. They can embrace Jesus as a Savior and Lord and ask him the hard questions too.

I want to encourage every leader, parent, and anyone who is around a child to read this. Stop and consider the questions Melissa asks at the end of each chapter and take one step forward to create safe places for kids to follow Jesus!

—Tom Bump
Coach, Speaker, Author, Pastor to Pastors with RestoringLeaders.org

Imagine you're sitting across from Mel in your favorite spot with a bottomless pot of your favorite drink. You've got all day to catch up, so you ask her to share some wisdom and growing pains. You both laugh. You both cry. And you both pause more than once to whisper a prayer. This book reads like a raw conversation from someone who's followed the Shepherd through the valleys and hills of children's ministry. For the new leader, it's a jackpot of timeless principles to grow the kids in your ministry. For the seasoned leader, it's a hallelujah and an amen to raising life-long disciples. And for the hardened leader, it's a gentle reminder of what matters most when all is said and done. Read it to receive, read it to refresh, read it to remember.

—Sarah Her
Discipleship Pastor
Life Transformation Church

Discipling World changers by Melissa J. MacDonald, provides a comprehensive roadmap for instilling faith, authenticity, and core beliefs in young minds. With a focus on pointing them to Jesus and equipping them with tools for life, MacDonald offers practical guidance for parents, pastors, and anyone who desires to positively impact the next generation.

MacDonald's genuine love for children shines through her writing. Through real-life ministry examples, Melissa shares with us the immense responsibility and privilege we have in shaping the lives of children. MacDonald's dream of raising a generation that changes the world is inspiring and challenging. This book is a must-read for anyone who seeks to make a lasting impact on young hearts and minds, empowering them to become lights in a world that needs their transformative influence.

—Corey Jones
Executive Pastor
Southern Hills, the Church at City Station

Melissa has written a deeply authentic, must-read guide for anyone looking to disciple today's kids. Packed full of heart felt stories and of examples of how to put Jesus at the center of it all, Melissa also encourages us to pause and reevaluate our role in the lives of Kids. Read this book... go beyond just information and step into discipling world changers!

—Michele Baird
Senior Director, Marketing
David C Cook

I have had the honor to walk with Melissa close up and also watch her develop as a Leader's Leader. Her new book *Discipling World Changers* is a game changer for any parent, child, or Ministry Leader. I've been asked to endorse a lot of books that just shine a spotlight on the issues and challenges of generational discipleship, but Melissa goes beyond shining a spotlight and offers practical answers that will give readers the results they are searching for. "Buckle up" and be reading to practice what Holy Spirit will reveal to you in these pages. Great job, Melissa, for obeying Jesus and creating this resource!

—Jim Wideman
Kidmin & Family Ministry Pioneer, Pastor, Author & Coach
jimwideman.com

Melissa's experience is a treasure trove for all who work in children's ministry. It was a joy to sit on the sidelines of this book, and listen to Melisa laugh, cry, implore, embrace, and challenge children for Christ. *Discipling World Changers* touches the heart of ministry: how to disciple children, turning their eyes upward and their hearts towards Jesus. It challenges you to look at your personal ministry and think through its effectiveness of it and encourages you to pray through how you can be a better disciple of children. *Discipling World Changers* gives practical tools and is a must-read for every children's leader and parent. It is a true inspiration.

—Debby Nalbandian
Director of Medallion
Jerusalem, Israel

Melissa's book, *Discipling World Changers,* needs to be gifted to every Kids Ministry Leader, whether new or seasoned. Melissa lets you into her world, experience, and heart as she takes the reader on an adventure of the wild blessing and profound cost of saying yes to Jesus for the sake of young world changers. She asks tough questions and invites you to dig deep as you give of yourself for the sake of the ones who have so much to offer, so much to share, and so much to do to build the Kingdom with us, for the sake of their own generation.

—Christie Penner Worden
Chief Mission Officer
RaiseUp Faith

Melissa beautifully reminds us that the purpose of every believer is discipleship. If we take Jesus' words to heart, we will make disciples. This isn't just limited to parents or ministers but every Christ follower. This is how we change the world. I read with tears in my eyes, remembering all the people on my journey who helped me become who God created me to be. Not only do we need each other, but our story and part in someone else's story matters. The ripple effect of your obedience goes further than you could ever imagine. Melissa teaches with an equal mix of transparency, humor, and wisdom. Her story will inspire us to change the world, one disciple at a time.

—Yancy Richmond
Songwriter, Worship Leader & Author
Yancy Ministries, Inc

As you read the pages, you inevitably identify with the authenticity Melissa infuses into every page. It becomes clear why teachers and kids adore her and appreciate her wisdom.

Melissa provides tools for developing world changers and demonstrates their ease of use. Beyond her brilliant insights and assistance, she reignites your love for kids all over again.

—Ron Hunter Jr. Ph.D.
author, speaker, and CEO of D6 Family Ministry

In *Discipling World Changers,* you will see and feel the heart of real-life ministry experiences from Melissa (Mrs. Mel). In a society that seems to be rift with abandoning children's true needs, Melissa gives us a gift, chock full of practical ways to raise up World Changers. Her heart for children, families, and Jesus comes through on every page. From her personal stories, the stories of families and children - whether told on the pages or through notecards - I was encouraged by the wisdom and guidance of someone gifted and called to help us raise World Changers. It is easy to feel the joy, challenges, heartbreak, and healing Mel presents throughout this text. Whether you are a parent, a children's worker, or a pastor, if you have a heart for children, families, and Jesus, this book is for you.

—Dr. Rich Griffith, Professor of Youth Ministry
Toccoa Falls College
Author: "Voices: Helping Our Children and
Youth Listen to Wise Counsel"

This is a timely book by Melissa MacDonald addressing an urgent need in today's Church which is experiencing a global family discipleship crisis. *Discipling World Changers* requires starting early and modeling humble listening and walking with Jesus in the everyday moments in life.

Melissa shares her own honest journey and struggles to help disciple the youth she loves and serves. She candidly provides what she has learned and seen bearing fruit in their young lives. As a parent or leader ministering to children, if you desire to disciple "World Changers", then you will find encouragement and equipping within in these pages.

We are co-laborers with God sowing and investing into young lives in the power of the Holy Spirit to be Jesus to them and see Jesus formed in them. It's a process that requires us to be committed and proactive, and we are as much changed by it as they are! Enjoy the read, the adventure, and the transformation!

—Harry Bryans, pastor, coach, EEA Children's Ministry
Associate, author of *The Generational Awakening*,
www.thegenerationalawakening.com

Melissa's ability to stitch theology with story and depth is a brilliant piece of written tapestry. A dose of timely humor and a nudge to live each day with eyes for discipleship makes her newest book so worthy to be read and practiced by myself and others. May it be so.

—Byron L. Ragains
David C Cook Field Representative

DISCIPLING
WORLD
CHANGERS

Raising Up a Generation That Changes the World Instead of the World Changing Them

Melissa J. MacDonald

END GAME
Press

End Game Press books may be purchased in bulk at special discounts for sales
promotion, corporate gifts, ministry, fundraising, or educational purposes.
Special editions can also be created to specifications. For details, contact
Special Sales Dept., End Game Press, P.O. Box 206, Nesbit, MS 38651 or info@
endgamepress.com.

Visit our website at www.endgamepress.com.

Library of Congress Control Number: 2023946642

Paperback ISBN: 9781637971260
eBook ISBN: 9781637971819

Cover by Dan Pitts
Interior Design by Typewriter Creative Co.

Printed in India
10 9 8 7 6 5 4 3 2 1

For my mom and dad who consistently model for me what radical, out-of-the-box, love-without-boundaries, always-point-to-Jesus, fight-hard-for-the-lost ministry looks like. The best parts of me are because of you.

Table of Contents

...you for being
... even ...
... every day even when
we don't see it.

I pray for my friend who
does not belive in God and
I want him to find him
in his life, please pray

My complaints are so small
compared to the lives of millions
of other people in the world I
will begin to pray + ask God
to help me stop complaining +
make a difference in the world.

God, you need control of me all the time even when I have time that I want to for me.

God I trust you to work in my life even when it's hard.

Introduction

"Miss Mel, you are literally the craziest person I have ever met. Your stories are crazy, and your life is crazy. But, I love you. Thank you for helping me understand who God is."

"I finally get it! Miss Mel, I finally get how much God loves me."

"I don't know why God let this happen, but I know he loves me."

"Can you pray for me so that I can love my mom more?"

"I've been learning more about trusting God."

"Now I know God loves me no matter what."

"God is with me always. Always."

Who doesn't love the heartbeat of a child? I mean, seriously. Their sweet openness never ceases to amaze me. They are honest—sometimes to a fault. They are eager to learn. They are moldable. They love without limits. They comfort without reason. And they forgive without excuses.

As a foster mom who just said, "Please don't use your teeth

to scratch me," I can admit that while incredible, kids are not perfect. They are not born basically good, and the world corrupts them. Every person is affected from the moment they are born because of Adam and Eve's sin in the garden. We are born with a sin nature, the evidence of such which can be seen from our earliest of days. Yet there is something about children. I have seen the face of God most often in the face of a child.

For those of us who work with kids, or those of you who parent children, it is an incredibly unique kind of sacred trust.

That God allows us to speak into and help mold the littlest of these continues to amaze me. Also, in the spirit of honesty, it scares me to death sometimes.

I so badly want to do everything right and make sure I prepare them the very best I can so they do well in this world. Not well by the world's standards but by God's standards. I want them to love the unlovable, be a light in dark places, wisely make hard choices, and love God more every day. And being faced with the reality that I can't *make* them do anything scares me even more. This sacred trust is immense. It's not about holding something but releasing someone. It's about molding and guiding and releasing. It's about Him.

For the last twelve years, I have spent every summer at camps with kids. The first time I was asked to be a camp speaker for kids other than my own, as a children's pastor, I said yes with fear and trembling. I knew I loved kids, and I knew I had something to say to them. I also knew that God would give me what I needed. What I did not know was how much speaking to kids at camp would not be about giving something to them but receiving something from them.

As I have loved on kids it has become my deep desire to become more like them. They exude the very character of God. Nobody loves like a child. I'm a self-professed overthinker. Perhaps it's my love of learning or my love of breaking molds, but whatever the case, the more I observe children, the more I think: Why aren't we as adults, more like children? Beyond that, what happens to us between childhood and adulthood that so changes how we love God and walk with Him? What can we do to change that?

I have this crazy dream. I'm no Martin Luther King Jr., but

I do have a dream. It involves our kids and the adults they will become. What if we raised up a generation of kids who happen to the world instead of the world happening to them? What if we raise up a generation of kids who change the world instead of the world changing them? What if we disciple a generation of world changers?

I've been accused of being naïve before and I probably will be again, but it doesn't distract me. A sincere deep-seated faith in the ability of God to do the seemingly impossible is often confused for naiveté. Our world needs fewer doubters and more people who exude the gift of faith. Faith often looks silly and is rarely popular. There is a fine line between being a realist and being a defeatist.

"God has not given us a spirit of fear, but of power and of love and of a sound mind." –2 Timothy 1:7 NKJV.

If I'm honest with you, I wish some truly unpopular things for kids and teens. I wish for them to be ugly until they're about twenty-five. I mean honestly, as soon as they get past the awkward stage and become handsome and beautiful, life just gets harder. I wish we could make them hermits until they're in their 20s and their brains are fully developed. I wish they could be exactly who they are without anyone ever making fun of them or questioning them. I wish they could be as weird and unique as they want without feeling hurt or betrayed. I bet if you were honest back to me, you might have some of these same wishes. They come from a good heart, but we all know they're not practical ideas.

Discipling world changers is not about hiding kids from the world but rather giving them the tools to *live* in this world. It means equipping them to be safe in their physical attractiveness, giving them wisdom to combat hurt, and allowing them to experience the world with a solid truth girding them from deception. It means preparing them for as much of this dark world as we can.

I believe God gave us one of His greatest gifts when He gave us children. I believe God is already using kids, and that He desires for us to release more kids into ministry instead of cloistering them in our homes. Our world is dark, and it isn't going to get lighter. It's not about hiding our kids from the world but equipping them to live in the world as Christ-followers. This is not about life skills. This is about *light* skills and raising up a generation of bright lights in a dark world.

That's my desire, my dream, and the calling God has placed on my heart. So whether you're a grandparent, parent, pastor, children's director, volunteer, auntie, or just know a kid, I invite you to dive in with me as we explore this idea of discipling world changers.

CHAPTER ONE

Faith

HEBREWS 11 IS KNOWN AS THE "FAITH" CHAPTER OF the Bible.

This section lists the great men and women of faith throughout biblical history, and it's probably my favorite chapter in the Bible. I love how some of the main characters in my favorite Bible stories were counted as faithful in spite of their imperfection. More often than not I think, "HOW did they get in there?"

God in His sweet infinite wisdom gives us a number of very clear examples of flawed people whom He found faithful. Rather than judging them by a single moment (good or bad), He looked at the whole and called them faithful.

I believe that when we work with kids we have to have a Hebrews 11 type of faith. It's so easy to get caught up in the day-to-day moments and either feel like failures or like winners when the fact of the matter is that discipleship is so much more than just a moment or a stage. It's life-on-life transformation. It doesn't stop at a certain age and it doesn't give up when things get too hard. It's walking in faith knowing that we serve a perfect God who will do what He has promised to do.

IN THE BIG AND SMALL MOMENTS

Twenty years ago I left the frozen tundra of Minnesota and boarded an airplane for Florida to do a youth ministry internship in Edgewater. I was thoroughly excited until I landed and realized how scary it was to be doing what I was doing. I landed in Orlando not knowing a single soul. I was picked up by my host family and driven toward the beach (thank you, Lord).

My internship was a mixture of emotions and experiences. I often chalked it up to a crash course on what not to do. In the midst of the fear over spiders the size of my hand that showed up in my shower and the frustration over working for an inexperienced youth pastor, God began to weave a love for people onto the fabric of my heart. These people became forever embedded into the story of who I am. Maybe somebody forgot to teach me that because I was doing a youth ministry internship, my ministry and love should have been limited to the age group I was serving? Or maybe I have a big heart and love easily. Or maybe, just maybe, God calls us to love for the long haul.

This chapter is being written on an airplane after visiting my Florida "home" which is how I refer to Edgewater even now, twenty years later. Last night "my kid" Davey came over. He's now in his 20s and married with a baby. It's rare for me to visit Florida and not see him. When I started my internship he was a precocious eleven-year-old who freely gave hugs, made me laugh, and had a kind word for everyone. Nothing has changed through the years. When Davey and his wife Christie were married, I was at the wedding cheering on their union. When I got the news that their first baby was stillborn, I pulled over and cried my eyes out in a grocery store parking lot. And when I got to hold their miracle baby last night, I kissed his little head and whispered a prayer of blessing over him. I think that this is more of what discipleship looks like. It's the nitty-gritty of life.

It's the big moments and the small moments. It's the eleven-year-old *and* the twenty-four-year-old.

RELEASING CONTROL

I've been in full-time ministry since 2003 when I took my first job right out of college as a children's pastor. Nobody told me that being a children's pastor would wreck my heart. I had grandiose dreams of helping shape kids and then moving them on to the youth ministry. Once they entered the youth ministry I would be done and ready to focus on the next round. Little did I know just how misinformed my dreams and ideas were. In all honesty, there are days when I wish loving people was that simple. It would be so much less messy.

In early summer several years ago, I was driving on a little highway in northern Idaho. Lake Pend Orielle was my view as tears streamed down my face. I was overwhelmed with so many things. I had just spent three days loving on some of my kids. I was their children's pastor when they were eight and now that they were in their late teens, I was a different type of pastor in their lives. Over countless coffee dates and ice cream dates we caught up and they shared with me, something we'd done for years. My common question was always, "How's your heart?" I prefer to get to the heart of the matter. I don't want to chit-chat. I want to connect.

As I was driving along the lake reflecting on those conversations, I was overwhelmed by God's grace in my life. My time as a children's pastor in Idaho was one of the most rewarding and difficult times of my life. I loved my kids, my team, and my church but the structure I was working within was, to put it lightly, tough.

The very way God had created and gifted me was seen as more of a threat than a blessing to some of my leadership. It was a difficult four years, but I came to understand more of who I was. God refined many of my rough edges and I can now look back and be grateful. However, the journey was not without some severe wounds inflicted by people I had trusted.

Almost ten years later, I drove through the same state thanking God for his grace. I was overwhelmed with gratitude for my story, for how God was designing the tapestry of my life. I was grateful for redemption and healing. And in the midst of the gratefulness, I was suddenly gripped with fear for my kids. Isn't that how it goes so often? We can't simply be grateful. We have to have something to worry about.

I pulled the car over at a turnout and sat staring at the lake as I continued to cry. Nobody told me that loving teens and young adults would take me to being a whole new level of prayer warrior. Hearing how my kids were doing and their openness (and for some of them, their lack of openness) made me ache for them.

My hands clenched so tightly that my nails dug into my palms as I beseeched God on their behalf. If I could have magically inserted Jesus into their lives, hidden them from the world, and made all of their choices for them I would have. The fear I had for them was so engulfing that I just wanted to control everything I could reach. My nails dug in deeper as I asked God why loving had to be so painful. I shook with sobs as I saw each kid's face and the potential pitfalls they would face and were already facing. Fear and desire for control had me so tense I almost couldn't breathe.

And then God broke through. In a still small voice He gently said, "Mel, how can you thank Me for your story in one breath and ask that I deny these sweet ones their story in the next?"

A simple soft question that changed everything. I let out a long breath as my body started to relax. He was right. As usual. Some of the best parts of me are because of my story and the refining work of God in my life. It was in the trials and the hurt that I came to know Jesus intimately and where His character was revealed. How could I not want that type of depth of relationship for my kids?

At the icky heart of it all was one of my age-old issues: control. As if the God of the universe wasn't trustworthy enough. As if I could really fix it all myself. I slowly began to unclench my hands and turn my palms up. I once again placed my kids in the hands of their Father, exactly where they needed to be. In surrender I held my palms open and said, "I trust you, Jesus."

FAITH THAT GOES BEYOND US

My favorite verse in Hebrews 11 is verse 13 of the New Living Translation (NLT). It says, *"All these people died still believing what God had promised them. They did not receive what was promised, but they saw it all from a distance and welcomed it. They agreed that they were foreigners and nomads here on earth."*

Did you catch that? All the great men and women of faith died believing what God had promised *but* not seeing it all in their lifetimes.

My friends, this journey of discipleship continues far beyond us. We won't see it all, in fact there are times we don't see much of anything at all. Sometimes faith is simply obediently putting one foot in front of the other. Sometimes faith is simply opening our hands in surrender to a God who doesn't change. Sometimes faith is the simple acknowledgement that our God is greater than we will ever be and that's a beautiful thing.

Discipling world changers is going to be messy. It is not going to fit onto a chart or a to-do list. At times it's going to wreck you and other times it's going to mold you. It's going to push the limits of what you've always been taught and it's going to challenge you. It's intentional and it's purposeful.

Discipling world changers also means knowing exactly whom you serve. We are here for God. To point our kids to Him. To equip and mold and release them to Him. He is in control, and we are not. He has plans to prosper them and not to harm them. This Jesus that gave his life for us is trustworthy. The same God who chose to count Moses and David and Rahab as faithful is the same God we serve today. So we walk forward in faith.

Hey Reader:
Take a minute and read Hebrews 11.

1. Who sticks out to you?
2. What or who do you need to surrender to God as you embark on this book journey?
3. Make a list here and then release them to our big God.

CHAPTER TWO

What is Discipleship?

DISCIPLESHIP IS A WORD THAT HAS ITS VERY ORIGINS in Christianity. In Matthew 28:18-20 NIV Jesus commands his disciples to go and make disciples. *"Then Jesus came to them and said, "All authority in heaven and on earth has been given to me. Therefore go and make disciples of all nations, baptizing them in the name of the Father and of the Son and of the Holy Spirit, and teaching them to obey everything I have commanded you. And surely I am with you always, to the very end of the age."*

As Christ-followers these verses are not optional. They are commands. If we truly believe that we are here on earth to serve Him, then our very lives revolve around this command.

THERE IS NO FORMULA

A disciple is a student. Someone who models their life after someone else. In our case, we model our lives after Jesus. We learn from Him, we follow His teaching, and we strive to be more like Him. As we are discipled, we disciple others.

We're imperfect and always will be until we reach Heaven. We are not going to get it right all of the time. That in and of itself can feel defeating but here's the deal: if we were perfect, we wouldn't need Jesus.

2 Corinthians 4:7 NLT, *"We now have this light shining in our hearts, but we ourselves are like fragile clay jars containing this great treasure. This makes it clear that our great power is from God, not from ourselves."*

How beautiful is it that God uses our fragility and our mess-ups to point people directly back to Him. He is never not done redeeming the story.

Perhaps one of the hardest things for us to understand is that discipleship—true and healthy discipleship—cannot be contained in a formula.

In the Christian world we have tried over and over again to make discipleship fit into a box, into an outline, into something we can touch and feel. And over and over again as we do that we contaminate discipleship. In our desire to contain it we dilute it. In our desire to make it fit into a box we stiffen it.

It makes sense, doesn't it? We love control and we love order. Even the most free-spirited people like things that make sense. The very essence of discipleship is Jesus. Let's be honest: Jesus was perfect and we are not. How could we think our formulas would actually work?

ZIGZAGS

So then, we have this fluid, organic, undefinable thing called discipleship. And while discipling means to teach and to train, and it sounds rather straightforward, those of us who work with kids know it's anything but direct.

I just spent the weekend with my family in a cabin in Northern Wisconsin. It was our annual Labor Day vacation. My three-year-old nephew and I went kayaking every day. He wanted to paddle without knowing how to paddle. I spent hours (I'm not kidding) helping him learn to paddle and, between you and me, he still doesn't know how.

First I used words. Then I used a visual. Then I made up a song: "start at the top and pull to the back." Finally, I had him on my lap with his tiny grubby hands next to mine on the paddle and we paddled together. Thinking I had finally taught him, I set him up on his own and ... he promptly curled up in between my legs and fell asleep.

This, my friends, is just how it goes. We could blame it on kids and their lack of attention span but I'm just as slow and zigzagging in my journey to learn as they are.

DISCIPLESHIP IS DOING LIFE TOGETHER

The best form of discipleship I have ever experienced happened when I did life together with my kid or mentor. It's when we move beyond words to real life. It's harder than a formula but it's more impactful.

If we are going to raise up a generation of world changers it means we have to be in it for the long haul. It means we're committed for the good, the bad, and the ugly. And there are times the bad and ugly will far outweigh the good. It means we press into Jesus with everything we have in us and we walk forward.

Discipleship is messy, gritty, complicated, inconvenient, and just plain hard. It is also beautiful, worth it, transformative, and precious. If you feel like you're on a roller coaster, good. You are right where you should be.

I thought I understood messy and hard but last year my husband I started doing foster care. Now I'm understanding brand new levels of messy and hard. We're foster parents and we're also passionate about partnering with families to keep kids out of foster care. Because of that we have started co-parenting with a struggling single mom. We do school drop-off and pick-up. We are on call for rides, tough conversations, and more. We have come in contact with more "at-risk" kids. I now operate a clothing closet out of my garage and the back of my car.

Because of that, God has given us a presence in the lives of many of our local families who are struggling.

On any given day my husband can be found opening the

door of our SUV at school drop-off while kids pour out like it's some kind of clown car. He yells after them, "You are kind, you are amazing, you are loved!"

On any given day I can be found pulling shoes out of the back of our car to give to a mom I know who is struggling. Or texting a friend to say I need two gallons of milk ASAP because I know a family who has none.

DISCIPLESHIP IS BEING LIKE JESUS

Is all of that discipleship? I would say it is. Is it formulaic? Absolutely not. I would, however, say it is exactly how Jesus would be spending His days. If you study the ministry of Jesus on earth, you'll find that He spent the majority of his time with the people where they were. He did not go to the temple to minister. He went to people's places of work, their homes, and their towns. He met their basic needs and showed them His tangible love.

I spent ten years as a children's disciplemaking specialist.

For ten years I traveled about two hundred days a year. I was in and out of churches, conferences, and meetings. I never relocated to "the office" because I was firm in my belief that if I was not serving in my local community then I was not worth listening to.

So while I traveled extensively, I always came back home. Home to "the neighbs", my neighbor girls who have literally journeyed over from next door since they were eight. Home to my community where I serve on a board to prevent child abuse. Home to my community of faith where I help disciple kids and families.

Hear me on this: discipleship does not look like me on a big stage speaking. It looks like me choosing to model my life after Jesus whether I am on a big stage or I am at home singing our foster child to sleep. The big stage may be given more importance by the world's standards, but I believe by God's standards my most important work is what I do at home.

Hey reader, be sure you are not defining your discipleship by the world's standards or even the church's standards. Tune your ear to the voice and character of Jesus and disciple from there.

Ask yourself these questions to check in:

1. Am I regularly spending time learning from Jesus?
2. Are the decisions I'm making daily guided by the way of Jesus or the way of the world?
3. As I disciple am I becoming more like Jesus or less like Jesus?

Who I Am Matters

THIS BOOK READS A LITTLE BACKWARDS ON PURPOSE. So often when we pick up a book we want to get right to the "doing" part. You picked this up because, hopefully, you love the idea of discipling world changers.

It would be easy to start with the how, but the reality is this: if you and I, as disciple-makers, are not first concerned with who we are, we are in danger of producing good work but not actually discipling. Our discipleship must be an outflow from what God has done and is doing in us. If we're going to disciple world changers, we absolutely must start with who we are as disciples. Discipleship is contagious. Let's make sure what we are living out is something we want others to catch.

CHAPTER THREE

Discipleship Starts with Me

WHO WE ARE MATTERS MORE THAN WHAT WE SAY.

In this journey to disciple world changers, we must not, cannot, forget to look at ourselves. It's easier to gloss over our own personal journey and jump to the list of things to do. It's more comfortable for sure. Being task-oriented feels good because we accomplish something. We can check things off of our list.

And yet there will never be a check mark next to those we disciple. Discipleship is a lifelong journey that often has more to do with what God desires to do in me than it does with what I desire to do in someone else.

The healthiest disciples are those who have walked alongside other messy disciples. You, in the midst of your mess and your struggle, are exactly who God desires to use. I would be remiss to not talk directly to you—and to myself—in this journey.

Discipleship always starts with my heart and with yours.

As you walk alongside those in the journey you must not forget to look up. I recently was in the Minneapolis airport. I was exhausted. I'm not a weepy person but you combine hunger and exhaustion and I become a mess. I was biting my lip to hold back the deluge of mess I could feel coming. Having been in that airport hundreds of times, I put my head down and focused on getting to my gate. I kept my head down on the train, I kept my head down on the escalator, I kept my head down while I trudged MILES (I also exaggerate when I'm tired) through the airport. I did not stop to look up until I got to my gate.

Instead of saying "Omaha" (my home airport) the display said, "Sioux City." I looked around in confusion and realized I had walked to not only the wrong gate but the wrong terminal. I'm proud to say I did not start crying immediately. One rather awkward sob and then I pulled my shoulders back and started the long walk back to the opposite end of the airport.

This time I kept my eyes up.

If discipleship is not to point others to Jesus then what is it for? And if we aren't remembering to look up and toward our Jesus on a regular basis then what good is our content? Our context? Our connection? We must remember to look up and keep our own connection with Jesus.

DON'T FORGET THE WONDER.

"I just don't get it. How could God love me so much He would die for me? It just doesn't make sense, Miss Mel. I haven't done anything for Him," said a shocked and confused seven-year-old. That little one could not get over that Jesus loved her so much He would die for her. She could not get over the wonder of it.

"Miss Mel, I slept last night for the first time ever without a bad dream! I woke up smiling. I cannot stop smiling ever since I started a relationship with Jesus yesterday. This feeling is amazing!" said the nine-year-old beaming boy to me. He could not get over the wonder of it all.

When was the last time the wonder of God's great love for you has overwhelmed you? When did it last stop you in your tracks? That you and I have access to the God of creation in the form of a personal relationship should be bringing us to our knees on a regular basis. That great gift never loses its shine or wonder. If you are not regularly allowing yourself to be in awe of God at work in your life, you will lose your wonder to the busyness of your days and the struggle of your weeks.

RAHAB

My favorite story in the Bible for when I need to rediscover my wonder is the story of Rahab in the book of Joshua. That may seem like an unlikely place to go, but I find delight in the fact that God uses unlikely people and places to remind me of the wonder of Him.

Rahab is a prostitute in the city of Jericho (Joshua 2:1). She is lower than low. She is a nobody who is either used by men or overlooked. Her house is in the most vulnerable spot in the city: the city walls. The Israelites have been away from the Promised Land for over four hundred years. They've been wandering in the desert for forty years on their journey back to God's place for them. God is about to do His most defining work in the historical story of the Israelites by allowing them to enter the Promised Land. It's a huge moment because it's the fulfillment of prophecy. And here comes Rahab to interrupt, or to maybe remind us of the real point of the story.

She tells the spies, *"For the Lord your God is God in heaven above and on the earth below"* (Joshua 2:11 NIV). She uses her mouth to declare that God is the one true God, and she wants to follow Him. She asks the spies to give her their promise that they will spare her and her family. The spies reply, *"Our lives for your lives!"* (Joshua 2:14 NIV) Did you catch that? The spies from God's chosen people have just offered their lives in exchange for the lives of a prostitute and her family from the enemy camp. "Our lives for your lives" shows us a glimpse—hundreds of years before Jesus would come to earth—of the kind of audacious move he would make on our behalf. These spies ascribed worth to Rahab, maybe for the first time ever in her life. She wasn't someone to be used, she was someone to be seen.

Fast forward to Joshua 6. The Israelites have crossed the Jordan River. The walls of Jericho have fallen after their obedient march. Joshua is about to establish himself as the young, new leader of the Israelites with instructions for conquering Jericho. It's a big moment, a huge moment. They have finally arrived. They have finally entered the land God had promised them. Imagine the excitement, the disbelief, the relief. God's chosen people are finally entering God's chosen land. Joshua takes a deep breath and yells out, *"Shout! For the LORD has given you the city! The city and all that is in it are to be devoted to the LORD. Only Rahab the prostitute and all who are with her in her house shall be spared, because she hid the spies we sent"* (Joshua 6:16-17 NIV).

I can imagine the ripple that went through the crowd. The whispers of, "What did he just say?" and "Did he say prostitute?" Oh, the wonder of this story. That God's first move for establishing His domain in the Promised Land would be to save a prostitute and her family.

You see, God has been and always will be in the business of seeing the ones we count as the least as the most precious in His sight. His first big move was to remind His people that He is a God of redemption, He is a God of second chances, and He is a God of wonder.

Perhaps the most beautiful part of the story comes in Joshua 6:23-25 where it says that they brought Rahab and her family out to live among the Israelites. They did not just rescue Rahab, they adopted her. She became family. In fact, she would find her place in the very lineage of Jesus. That is the God who we serve. That is the God from whom our wonder should flow.

If you aren't regularly in awe of the God who loves you, how will you pass that on to the next generation? Don't forget your wonder.

DON'T FORGET THE TRUTH

I want this book to constantly take you back to God's word.

If we're going to point others to the Bible, then we must be in it ourselves. It's not enough for us to have nice ideas about who God is and what the Bible says, we must know His word *intimately*. We must align ourselves with it. It should be what keeps us grounded. Our experiences and emotions will lie to us over and over again, but truth remains sturdy and trustworthy. Matthew 24:35 NLT says, *"Heaven and earth will disappear, but my words will never disappear."*

What do you know to be true about God? Who is this God you serve? Our grounding starts there.

2 CORINTHIANS 4

For the last decade I have spent a lot of time meditating on 2 Corinthians 4. It has resonated with me so deeply and personally that it's been pivotal in molding me.

The journey I've been on for the last fifteen years could be a whole other book. I've been battling a debilitating disease and have fought off death more than once. It has been equal parts awful and beautiful. It has shaped me into who I am. I have both hated it and loved it. It has humbled me in ways I never would have thought possible, and it has given me a perspective that I treasure. I cling to the truth I find in 2 Corinthians. This might not be where you land, but start here and go digging into God's word for your own resonance.

2 Corinthians 4:1 NLT, *"Therefore, since God in his mercy has given us this new way, we never give up."*

I will not give up. God is merciful and I'm here for Him and I won't give up.

2 Corinthians 4:5 NLT, *"You see, we don't go around preaching about ourselves. We preach that Jesus Christ is Lord, and we ourselves are your servants for Jesus' sake."*

My message should never be about me. It should be about Jesus. I am His servant. My message should be His message and should always point others to Him.

2 Corinthians 4:7 NLT, *"We now have this light shining in our hearts, but we ourselves are like fragile clay jars containing this great treasure. This makes it clear that our great power is from God, not from ourselves."*

I am not perfect. And that is okay. My imperfections and fragility are not problems. They are opportunities for God to show His power.

2 Corinthians 4:8-11 NLT, *"We are pressed on every side by troubles, but we are not crushed. We are perplexed, but not driven to despair. We are hunted down, but never abandoned by God. We get knocked down, but we are not destroyed. Through suffering, our bodies continue to share in the death of Jesus so that the life of Jesus may also be seen in our bodies. Yes, we live under constant danger of death because we serve Jesus, so that the life of Jesus will be evident in our dying bodies."*

This life is a struggle. It is never going to be easy and yet in the struggle there is victory and there is beauty. We are not crushed. We are not driven to despair. We are never abandoned by God. We are not destroyed. These promises have literally carried me at times. Jesus is evident in the struggle. No struggle is wasted.

2 Corinthians 4:13 NLT, *"But we continue to preach because we have the same kind of faith the psalmist had when he said, 'I believed in God, so I spoke.'"*

I love the simplicity of this verse. I have wanted to give up more times than I can count, and it has been my faith in my God that has pulled me through. Whether I am sick or tired or heavy-hearted I keep going, speaking, and preaching because I believe in God. Simple and powerful.

2 Corinthians 4:16-18 NLT, *"That is why we never give up. Though our bodies are dying, our spirits are being renewed every day. For our present troubles are small and won't last very long. Yet they produce for us a glory that vastly outweighs them and will last forever! So we don't look at the*

troubles we can see now; rather, we fix our gaze on things that cannot be seen. For the things we see now will soon be gone, but the things we cannot see will last forever."

Again, we never give up. We're created for more. In the light of glory, these temporary aches and challenges are worth pushing on. I keep my gaze fixed on Jesus and I remember I'm here for more than just now. I'm here to make a lasting impact. I'm here for Him.

WHAT DO I KNOW TO BE TRUE?

In the midst of our foster care journey, we have had some very hard and scary days. One such day started with an unexpected email that took my breath away. The e-mail's implications for the child currently living with us were staggering. I called for my husband, Luis, who came running into my office upon hearing the panic in my voice. We read the email together, then I started losing it. I couldn't take full breaths and my eyes were full of tears. My husband and I grabbed each other in a tight hug. I forced out, "What do we know to be true?" with my face in his shoulder.

With tears in his eyes he pulled me back to look at him, "God is in control."

I nodded. "God is present."

"God loves our foster child more than we do."

"God does miracles."

"God is for us."

We went back and forth like this, naming God's promises until we could both breathe again. It did not change the email, but it did change our response to the email. We purposely realigned ourselves with truth and in that truth, we found a place to breathe. In that truth we were ministered to by God Himself.

To help ground others in the truth, you must first be grounded in truth yourself. You must breathe it in and out. You must be in it daily. You must be aware of it and intentionally connected with it. It must be where you start and where you end. Discipleship is nothing without the centrality of truth.

DON'T FORGET TO BE AWARE

In the middle of 2020, I started praying differently. I stopped asking God for things and started asking God to help me be more aware of Him. Let me explain. I used to pray things like, "God, join me here," or "Jesus, be very near to my friend tonight," or "God, help me with this problem." I realized those prayers were coming from an assumption that God was not already present, which was bad theology. Because I have a relationship with Jesus I can be assured of His presence (Psalm 139:7 NLT). Because God loves to draw near to His people, I can be assured He is present (James 4:8 NLT).

In light of that, I started praying with the knowledge that God was already present and I needed help to be aware of His presence. "God, I know you are with me today, please make me aware of Your work in my day." And, "Jesus, even when I feel like You are distant, I know You are near. Help me to be aware of Your nearness today."

The change in my prayer life has been significant. I start by remembering the wonder, I ground myself in the truth of Scripture, and then I work on being aware of His presence. He is always at work around me, and I need to be watching for it. I find I am so much more aware of God's presence throughout my day. Instead of operating from a deficit of needing God's presence, I operate from an overflow of God's ever-steady presence already in my life.

In 2022 I took it one step further and I decided to purposefully practice thankfulness. Every night (well, most nights) I grab my journal and I write down at least five things I am thankful for from the day. The things I write down are tangible evidence of God's presence. The discipline of writing them down causes me to pause in stillness and be aware of His presence, and in that beautiful circle I am grounded in truth and reminded of the wonder. In short, this daily practice causes me to look up to make sure I'm connecting with my Father.

Hey reader, discipleship starts with you. Look up. Psalm 121:1-2 NLT says, *"I look up to the mountains—does my help come* *from there? My help comes from the LORD, who made heaven and earth!"*

Ask yourself these questions to check in:

1. Am I filled with wonder? What story or scripture reminds me of the wonder?
2. Am I regularly grounding myself in truth? Make a list of God's promises that are especially dear to you.
3. Am I aware? Am I operating with the knowledge that God is present and I need to be aware of Him?

CHAPTER FOUR

Our Role

THIS BOOK HAS A TWO-PERSON AUDIENCE. THOSE OF you serving kids and families in a church setting and parents/caregivers of children. Ideally, both audiences should go hand-in-hand.

Parents, we as ministry leaders are here to serve you, validate you, and come alongside you. Ministry leaders, hear me say this, we are here to *serve* parents, *validate* parents, and *come alongside* parents. Let's make sure we do not reverse our roles and think parents are here to serve us, validate us, and come alongside us.

THE SUNDAY SCHOOL MOVEMENT

The Sunday school movement began in 1780s Britain.

Due to the Industrial Revolution, children worked long

hours in factories to provide for their families. Some kind-hearted Christians saw this and wanted to make sure these children were not illiterate. Because they were working six days a week, Sundays were the only days that children could actually go to school.

Thus "Sunday school" began. By the mid-19th century Sunday school was a regular part of childhood. In *Christianity Today,* Timothy Larsen writes, "Even parents who did not regularly attend church themselves generally insisted that their children go to Sunday school. Working-class families were grateful for this opportunity to receive an education. They also looked forward to annual highlights such as prize days, parades, and picnics, which came to mark the calendars of their lives as much as more traditional seasonal holidays."

Sunday school always included a religious aspect. The Bible was used as a textbook in many cases and morals and virtues were taught to children. After state education came onto the scene by the 1870s, Sunday School transitioned to strictly religious education. But Sunday school had already become ingrained as a regular weekly rhythm. It wasn't until the 1960s that Sunday school began to be seen as optional for many children.

I bring this up is because it's important for us to understand that children's ministry was originally born out of a need to take care of children's education. Along the way it morphed into religious education and became a part of church tradition. Times have changed. Culture has shifted and roles have shifted and yet the church has had a hard time adjusting. Ministry leaders, the time has come for us to reevaluate our roles in kids's lives. Do we still have a role? Yes, but it may look different and that is okay.

AN APOLOGY

I want to pause here for a moment to apologize to the parents.

As a church leader I want to apologize to you on behalf of the church. As the Sunday school movement shifted, the church sent the message that its leaders were more important than you. We developed an over-inflated view of ourselves. We thought we were first in your children's spiritual development, and that you were secondary. We threw up our hands in frustration as your church attendance declined and we did not get the time we thought we needed with your children to teach them the way of Jesus. We sent papers home and complained when we found them discarded in the parking lot. We touted the need for you to be in church for the spiritual development of your kids without pausing to acknowledge your own role in their journey. We made it seem like you were incapable of leading the way in your children's spiritual formation. We made many of you feel like your influence came second to the church. We were, and are, wrong.

I humbly apologize for cutting you off at the knees and sending the message that you are inadequate. You, parents and caregivers, are the number one spiritual influencers in your kid's life. You, not us. You lead the way in your children's spiritual life whether you feel equipped to do that or not. Forgive us for trying to take on a role that God designed you to have. Forgive us for not coming alongside you to equip you. Forgive us for thinking too highly of ourselves.

LET'S COME TOGETHER

If we're going to raise up a generation that changes the world we're going to have to join together. The pandemic was a reality check for both parents and the church. We need each other. For spiritual development neither of us is expendable. I believe there is still a place for both parents and the church to work together. The importance of fellowship with other believers in community is mentioned time and time again in the Bible.

Hebrews 10:25 NLT says, *"And let us not neglect our meeting together, as some people do, but encourage one another, especially now that the day of his return is drawing near."*

1 John 1:7 NLT tells us that, *"if we are living in the light, as God is in the light, then we have fellowship with each other, and the blood of Jesus, his Son, cleanses us from all sin."*

We need to be in fellowship with one another. Parents, you need to be in fellowship and your kids do as well. I'd like to propose that we from the church world begin working alongside parents instead of treating you like you're expendable.

TO CHURCH LEADERS

Take a deep breath and receive some observations.

I cannot tell you how many times I hear complaints about parents (I have been guilty of them as well):

"They never take home the sheets we give them."
"None of them ever volunteer."
"They drop their kids off late and don't remember to pick them up on time."
"They're inconsistent."
"They don't care what we teach their kids."

Please, my friends, stop complaining. We are not here to fight against parents, we are here to fight *for* parents. We are here to strengthen and support the role God has given them (Catch that—God gave them this role. Be careful that you are not trying to take away what God gave them.). Our job is to come alongside them, to be their biggest cheerleaders, their most skillful helpers, their strongest prayer warriors, and their most compassionate listening ear.

Your understanding of your job must change to equipping, empowering, and elevating parents (please note, when I say parents, I mean any full-time caregiver of children).

I'm new to parenting, and foster parenting is complicated. With that being said, I can't fully speak for all parents, but I do talk to many and this is what they're saying:

- Many of them are trying their best but they feel like they're flying blind. The pandemic revealed to them that they matter in their children's spiritual development, but they feel like they do not have the needed tools for the role.

- They want the church to help them parent.

- They want the church to see their kids, not just try to keep them distracted and quiet.

- They want the very best for their kids.

- Even if they aren't sure about Jesus, they want their kids to have good morals and character.

- They appreciate you but the reality is you are not nearly as important to them as you think you are. You have their kids for an hour every week (if they come every week) and they have them the rest of the time. They don't need a quick fix on a Sunday morning, they need tools to be quality parents the rest of the week.

May I suggest a few things?

1. **Create a prayer list of your ministry kids's parents.** Kids's ministry encompasses the whole family, whether it's called family ministry or not. Start praying over the parents in your ministry.

2. **Humble yourself.** What you do is awesome and important but the spiritual growth and development of the kids in your ministry does not rise and fall on you alone. They belong to God, and they belong to their parents. After that we get to love on them and point them to Jesus.

3. **Rethink what you do.** Would you begin to breathe grace in and out over the parents of your kids? Would you ask them how you can be praying for them? Would you ask them how you can bless them? Would you write them notes of encouragement? Would you consider changing your ministry to a little less kid-focused and a little more family-equipping-focused?

4. **Don't forget the kids.** On the heels of all of the above I want to encourage you to not forget the kids you get to love on. For some of these kids you may be the bright spot in their week, you might be the one who introduces them to Jesus, and your church might be the only place they feel safe. Don't forget that.

I'm often reminded that in our desire to equip the family we cannot forget the kids who either don't have families or who have families that don't care what their kids do. Nearly every week at my little home church in Iowa we have kids wander across the street from the trailer court. Their parents kinda know where they are, kinda know what they're doing, and kinda don't care. They walk across the street and are enveloped and loved for the small time we have them. Don't forget the kids.

TO PARENTS

Let us in. We love your kids, we love you, and we desire for your kids to love Jesus. It really does take a village. May we be a part of your village? In the book *Sticky Faith,* Chap Clark and Kara E. Powell talk about the ratio of 5:1. Kids need their faith to be sticky, meaning it needs to stick. They have a greater likelihood of their faith being sticky if they have a ratio of 5:1 in their lives. Five adults invested in your kid's life. Five adults, outside of you, who love your kids, pray for your kids, cheer for your kids, mentor your kids, and spur your kids on. God never intended for you to be the only person your child needs in their life. You are created for community and your kids are as well. Let us in.

I made my way from Southwest Iowa to the city of Sandpoint, Idaho as a children's pastor who loved, prayed for, cheered on, mentored, and spurred on the kids in my ministry in 2016. My Madi girl was graduating from high school. I've been Madi's pastor since she was about eight. We've done a lot of life together and there was no way I could miss her graduation. I squeezed in next to her dad and joined the family crew there to cheer on her commencement on a foggy day in June. I exchanged teary glances with her parents and choked up when I saw her march up the aisle in her hat and gown.

My mind skipped back in time to cheering her on at her soccer game when she was ten. We went to ice cream when she was eleven to talk about a friend who had hurt her. Retreats, family game nights, school visits, plays, and more. After moving away, I Skyped in for her first homecoming date. I met the date over Skype and had a "talk" with him. In eighth grade she saved up all her money to come visit me. I've been back intentionally to visit every year to check in with her, ask her tough questions, hold her accountable, meet the boyfriends, meet the friends, and have talks long into the night while sitting by the lake.

I have watched countless soccer games and basketball games online cheering her on from whatever city I was in that day. We've "snapped each other", texted each other, and called each other. She's called me crying and called me excited. I've walked with her.

Here's the beauty of why I was allowed to do all of that: her parents let me in. From the very beginning they recognized Madi and I had a special bond. They encouraged that bond. They wanted other people in her life who would speak into her life and point her to Jesus. There has never been any jealousy but rather a sense of teamwork. We've been in it together. As I hugged them and we took a "family" picture together all sorts of tears flooded my eyes. She wasn't my kid but I get to be a part of her story. There is nothing sweeter.

Madi is a middle school English teacher today. The relationship continues. All because her parents let me in. Parents, be on the lookout for people you can trust with your kids. Let them in. You are not meant to do this alone. Allow us to speak words of truth into your child's life. Allow us to walk alongside you in this adventure.

World changers have people in their lives whom they can trust, whom they can respect, and who work as a team. It is time for the church and parents to join hands and do this together. There is no battle against you, only teamwork. Our kids need to see this modeled and lived out on a regular basis. Let's show them what healthy looks like.

Hey Reader: Pause for a moment. What are you taking away from this chapter?

1. Parent, what do you need to receive?
2. Leader, what you do need to receive?
3. We need each other. How can you reach out in kindness and support today?

CHAPTER FIVE

Spiritual Health

As ADULTS WHO DESIRE TO DISCIPLE WORLD CHANG-
ers, it is important that we practice working toward spiritual
health. Kids desperately need to see adults who are willing to
do the hard work to become better versions of themselves. They
do not need us to be perfect, but they do need to see that we
are intentionally and willingly striving toward spiritual health.
It's important that we model for them what that looks like.

At the ripe age of twenty-three I burned out. I can't even say
it was a slow burn, it was rather explosive.

The pastor I was serving under was a challenge. I was working on my master's degree, and my children's ministry had
grown from fifty kids to 250 in under a year. I didn't think it was
possible to burn out so young, so I brushed it off as a learning
curve or an adjustment period. But it was burnout, plain and
simple. In my desire to serve Jesus I had lost connection with

Him. Turns out you can burnout even while doing really good things for Jesus.

Life moved on. I switched jobs, and I intentionally spent quality time with Jesus. I began to mend. I didn't exactly know what had gone wrong, but I did know I didn't want to go back to that point ever again. Imagine my shock when three years later, in a whole different church, I found myself at the point of burnout yet again. Fortunately, this time I had tools and wise people in my life, and I began to recognize some of the unhealthy habits I had.

DEFEATING THE LIES

Somewhere along the way I had begun listening to and operating out of Satan's lies. Those lies told me I was only as good as what I could do. They told me that my performance mattered more than my soul, that my worth was tied up in my accomplishments. They told me that I was too loud. They told me I was too strong. They told me that I wasn't cut out for ministry because I never seemed to fit in anywhere.

Ever been there?

I knew all the right answers to tell other people, but I didn't know how to personally deal with those lies. During a spiritual formation class as a part of my master's program, I had to write out the lies that played over and over in my head. I took the space to make that list and it was long. Next to the lies I wrote a truth right out of the scripture.

Lie: "I'm only worth what I can accomplish."

Truth: 2 Timothy 1:9 NLT, *"For God saved us and called us to live a holy life. He did this, not because we deserved it, but because that was his plan from before the beginning of time—to show us his grace through Christ Jesus."*

Lie: "I'm not cut out for ministry."

Truth: Isaiah 41:9 NLT, *"I have called you back from the ends of the earth, saying, 'You are my servant.' For I have chosen you and will not throw you away."*

Lie: "I need people to affirm what I do."

Truth: Colossians 3:23-24 NLT, *"Work willingly at whatever you do, as though you were working for the Lord rather than for people. Remember that the Lord will give you an inheritance as your reward, and that the Master you are serving is Christ."*

Lie: "God can't possibly fix this mess."

Truth: Ephesians 3:20 NLT, *"Now all glory to God, who is able, through his mighty power at work within us, to accomplish infinitely more than we might ask or think."*

Lie: "I wish God would stick with my plan!"

Truth: Isaiah 55:8-9 NLT, *"'My thoughts are nothing like your thoughts,' says the Lord. 'And my ways are far beyond anything you could imagine. For just as the heavens are higher than the earth, so my ways are higher than your ways and my thoughts higher than your thoughts.'"*

My list went on and on. I gave my lies to God and then I intentionally began to combat them as they came into my head. As the lies came in, I would quote scripture and truth. Slowly but surely, I began to hear truth instead of the lies. It was not an overnight win. It was a long battle. In fact, I still do this exercise. The enemy is never done with us, and we can't be done fighting him just because things get a little better. I must purposely put truth into my head and heart.

SELF-AWARENESS AND SPIRITUAL HEALTH

In the little Christian college I attended it seemed as if all the *very* spiritual people got up early to do their devotions. I would see them bent over their Bibles and journals as I was brushing my teeth and running across the lawn to my early class.

I wanted to be very spiritual, I really did. But I wanted sleep even more. I tried to set my alarm for 6 a.m. and found that when it went off at 6 a.m. I did not have even a remotely spiritual feeling. In fact, it made me angry. A mentor graciously pointed out to me that I needed to stop trying to do what I thought was spiritual and start being who God created me to be.

My mind was blown! You mean I could do my devotions at night before I went to bed, and it would work just as good? It would actually work even better because I liked my time with Jesus at night (I did not enjoy time with Jesus at 6 a.m.).

We serve and are loved by a personal God. This means the more aware of who I am, the better I understand God. Self-awareness is key for unlocking spiritual health. When I know who I am, I am better able to understand how God designed me. It's a beautiful thing to be known intimately by our Creator.

My self-awareness journey has led me to a few things I strive to do in my spiritual journey.

Give myself grace. I am my own worst enemy. Nobody judges me more harshly than I do. When I look around, I realize that I am the only person holding me to impossibly high standards. When I do that, I fall right back into the trap of lies that tells me my performance and perfection matter. When I start to see myself falling back into that trap, I ask myself four questions.

1. Have I done the best I could with what I had to work with?
2. Was I sensitive to the Holy Spirit and did I allow Him to interrupt me?
3. Did I answer "no" to either of the two above questions? If yes, talk to Jesus about it. Confess and receive His grace.
4. Did I answer "yes" to the above? If so, receive grace and go in peace.

Stop comparing. For far too long I measured my spiritual success by what I thought others's "success" looked like. How long could I be silent in a prayer retreat (the answer is about five minutes)? How often did I journal? How many verses did I have memorized?

I am intentionally striving to stop comparing myself to

others and to start embracing me. Instead of using others as a measuring stick, I look to God and who He created me to be. I find that me being me brings joy to my Father, and we delight in each other.

Say "no." A common phrase I repeat to myself is, "Just because I can doesn't mean I should." There are a lot of things I can do, and there are a lot of things I love to do but that does not mean I should say yes to everything. "Because I can," is not an answer for why I'm doing something. I don't need to do it all. I do need to say no sometimes. Lately, God has been telling me that just because I love something doesn't mean I need to do it all the time. I love people and I love my job, but that does not mean I need to be *all* things to *all* people *all* the time. So I say no. I intentionally say yes and I intentionally say no.

Regularly seek wise counsel. I took a job in 2010 that required me to enter an intensive three days of counseling. I went kicking and screaming after begging God to release me from my job. He was rather firm in His "no" answer to that prayer. My masters is in counseling so it's not like I was opposed to idea, I had just been repeatedly wounded and betrayed by counselors.

In the middle of the great state of Nebraska I met a husband and wife and started the three days of counseling. Their first words to me were, "Tell us your story." I was so completely disarmed by that statement that I forgot I had decided ahead of time that I wasn't going to like them. I shared my story, and they showed me God's thread of grace throughout it. They spoke healing and forgiveness and purpose into my wounds, and I was changed forever. They became lifelong friends and to this day I meet with them regularly. I literally go to them, figuratively throw everything on the table, and they help me sort it through. They admonish me, speak truth over me, encourage me, correct me, and spur me on.

Schedule time to pause. I run at a fast pace. Part of it is my personality and part of it is my job. Either way it's not always healthy and if I'm not careful it can feed into my unhealthy need for performance. If I do not schedule time to pause, I will run out of time to do it. Right now, in my work life, that looks like not scheduling calls on Mondays. Those days can be used for work, or they can be used at my discretion in order to pause. In my personal life my pause moments are often found once our foster child goes to school. I brew good coffee, settle my puppy in my lap, and sit down with my Bible to pause and hear from God.

Ask good questions of myself. As a recovering workaholic and performance-driven person I intentionally ask myself questions to check in. "How is your heart?" This question always makes me think and do a gut check. How am I really? How I answer is often an indicator of what I need to do next.

Before I say yes to a speaking engagement or a new opportunity, I ask myself, "What is your motivation behind saying yes?" If my motivation is because people will notice, or it will make people happy or because I'll feel good about myself, I usually need to either say no or have a "Come to Jesus" moment.

"What has God been teaching you lately?" If I don't have an answer or my answer is from six months ago, I know it's time to be more intentional in my listening and responding to God.

Do things that feed my soul. There are certain things that make my heart happy. Like, really happy. I've learned that those are things that feed my soul. Jesus cares about my soul (Psalm 23), and so should I. Here are some things I do to tend to my spirit:

- Rent the convertible. (I love driving with the top down.)
- Sing really loudly. (Preferably in the convertible.)
- Find the beach. (If I'm traveling and there is a beach nearby, I will find it.)
- Chase the sunsets.
- Buy the good coffee.
- Takeout good ethnic food.
- Go thrift shopping.
- Dance in the kitchen with my handsome hubby.
- Take long walks in the fall and crunch all the leaves.
- Book the trip to Whidbey Island. (My favorite place.)

- Go work at the coffee shop with the really good coffee and the big windows where the sun streams in.

- Put worship music on, especially when the day is hard.

What would you put on your list?

I've never seen perfect a day in my life. Rather than perfection I pray my life is marked by my intentionality toward spiritual health. I want the world changers I'm discipling to see that. Me being me with all my quirks and imperfections tells my potential world changers that God uses the unlikely and God delights when we are exactly who He created us to be.

Hey Reader: Spend some time thinking through the lies you listen to. Ask God to help reveal those to you. Write down the lies and then combat them with scripture.

_____

_____

_____

_____

_____

_____

_____

_____

_____

_____

_____

_____

CHAPTER SIX

Authenticity

AUTHENTICITY IS SOMETHING I WILL NEVER STOP talking about. This book would not be complete without me spending some time talking about the importance of authenticity. Our world is loud and much of it is contrived to make the picture look better—or worse, depending on who is contriving it. This generation of kids today sees it all and knows there is something missing.

They are hungry for authenticity.

In a world that is crowded with inauthentic messages and people, kids are crying out for something real. They want to feel something that matters, and more importantly, they want to see *you* feel something that matters. We could easily say this is a "kid-only" heart-cry but in reality, all of us long to know and be around authentic people.

When we're authentic, people are able to make a connection

with us. The pedestal we might have been on before is gone and we are just like them. When we find common ground, we can suddenly learn from each other.

One summer at a camp, a little girl came up to me. She said, "Miss Mel, I used to think my life was crazy and then I met you and your life is way worse." I was so thankful she said that. She knew I was safe because I had let her into my own life. Because of that she found common ground and with common ground came her willingness to trust me, to let me in.

AUTHENTICITY IS ALWAYS RETURNED

Authenticity is always returned with authenticity. Always. Let that serve as both an encouragement and a warning to you. If you are honest and open with people, they will be open and honest with you.

Kids especially need someone they can be real and honest with. There is something unique about kids that they are so hungry to be real, but they won't do it with just anyone.

When I share kids's stories with adults, I always get asked, "Why did they talk to you? How did you make that happen?" Ideally, we'd all like a quick formula to get kids to open up to us. The reality is it's much easier than a formula. It's simple authenticity. Authenticity tears down walls better than anything else I have ever seen. The best way I know to illustrate the importance of authenticity is through stories.

One summer during a week I was speaking at a camp, my toddler nephew (who lived three hours from the camp I was at) had a grand mal seizure. It was the first time he had ever had a seizure. He proceeded to have another one a few hours later and was admitted to the hospital. This auntie was a wreck, I mean a *wreck*.

Everything in me wanted to get in my car and drive to him to kiss him and hug him. Yet I knew I was where I needed to be. Just as I was getting up to speak at the evening service, I got a text that he was seizing again. I was broken. I weaved my way through the kids sitting on the ground and found myself standing before them barely holding my emotions in check. In that moment I made a decision. I could fight through it, or

I could be authentic and allow them to enter into my journey. I decided to be authentic. I told them about my nephew who was having seizures.

I told them I was scared and sad and then I asked if anyone wanted to pray for my nephew. At least fifteen hands shot up. I picked three of the kids and they prayed, putting into words what my soul was aching. Their prayers were so utterly precious. I had tears in my eyes. When they were done, I said "Thank you" and dove into my message. Throughout the week it felt like every single kid at one time or another came to check on me and my nephew. And then because I had shared my fears and my journey with them, they began to share with me. They would find me at a meal or knock on my cabin door or ask to go canoeing, then they would share their own stories of fear and doubt. And during it all God was present and working.

AUTHENTICITY CREATES SAFE PLACES

At another camp I was sharing with young campers about choosing to trust God. I don't think my message on this particular night had anything to do with why Eva* (name changed) came and spoke to me when the message was over (often it has a lot less to do with our message than it does with our methods).

Eva came up afterwards, sat on one of the stage steps and started sobbing. Giant, ugly sobs were coming out of the little eleven-year-old. I could tell she wasn't trying to be dramatic or draw attention to herself. She just sat there crying without stopping. I sat by her silently, rubbing her back and passing her tissues. And then she began to talk to me. In the next hour she told me her story.

When I say authenticity is always returned with authenticity, I am serious and sometimes that truth is ugly. Eva's story nearly brought me to my knees more than once. She shared multiple forms of abuse she was experiencing. The more she told, the worse it got. She knew Jesus and loved him, but her story was hard. So hard. I had been her speaker at camp for three years in a row and she told me she finally knew she could trust me to tell her story to. We prayed together and I walked her to her cabin. I knew the next day I would have to report it all, but for that moment, that evening, I was spent. I was exhausted from the battering my soul took. I was angry beyond words. I was grateful that I knew she would sleep safe that night.

Because I had been authentic with a group of kids, Eva knew she could be authentic with me. Can I be honest?

In my selfishness I wish she hadn't been authentic with me. I wish I hadn't been the person she made her outcry to. I wish I hadn't had to watch her relive everything as she remembered. I wish I hadn't been the one to sit by her as she told her story to the authorities. It was beyond hard. I cried hundreds of tears with her.

In spite of how hard it was, when I step back, I'm so grateful she talked to someone. When I step back, I can see it really was not about me but about a little girl finding a safe, authentic person she could be honest with. I'm so grateful I was that person for her. I'm so grateful I could rub her back and hold her hand and pass her tissues as she cried a river of poison out of her. I'm so grateful my heart broke with hers. I'm so grateful I serve a sovereign God who sees, knows, and loves Eva even more than I do. I'm so grateful I was authentic and was able to step into her story for such a time as that. I'm so grateful.

AUTHENTICITY POINTS TO JESUS

Authenticity is a powerful tool and in its very essence is an inability to be false. There is no such thing as false authenticity, it's just a lie.

This generation can spot a lie from a mile away. They see right through us when we try to fabricate authenticity or attempt to use someone else's authenticity as our own. Authenticity means you intentionally give people a glimpse into your soul. That may sound scary but when we know Who we serve it really isn't scary at all. God is in the business of using our brokenness to glorify Himself.

When we live out an authentic life and story, we tell this generation that it's okay to not be perfect.

A number of years ago I was at Lake Swan Camp in Florida. It had been a long summer hearing hard stories. One night the line of kids who wanted to share their story with me was long. Each story was tough. The last little girl was a sweet as could be.

She started crying and with all honesty said, "Miss Mel, I've started a relationship with Jesus. I just want a different life." Her honesty flabbergasted me for a minute. She began to tell me her story of drug-using parents and how she was now living with her grandparents who weren't well. "Miss Mel, what happens when they die? Nobody wants me."

In my head I was throwing everything I owned out of my suitcase and creating a spot for her. She was little, she would fit, I was sure of it! My heart was broken for her. We prayed together and some of her little friends came and hugged her and prayed for her. As they walked out, I felt my whole body slump in defeat. I was done. I couldn't do it anymore. I walked to my car and sat in it. I started ugly crying. I railed at God for a few minutes, "How do you expect me to tell them about You in light of that? I can't do it, it doesn't fit. It doesn't work. I can't do this anymore."

I so badly wanted to fix it and I couldn't. So I did the logical thing, I told God I was quitting. After I quit, I sat there crying and saying, "God, I don't understand You but I trust You. I'm a little mad at You right now but I trust You."

I made it back to my cabin and texted my prayer team telling them I needed prayer. I didn't sleep well that night because I was wrestling with God.

The next morning, I found myself back in the chapel as they were introducing me. I stood in the back having an argument with God. "I quit. I'm done. I already told You this." He had tried gentle and now He just skipped to the point: "Get your butt up there."

Once I got over my shock that the Lord would use the word "butt", I trudged up front. I turned and looked at all those precious kids and I made a decision. I decided to be honest. I told them I had had a rough night. "I love that you share your stories with me, but they hurt my heart. My heart was hurting last night. I told God I trusted Him, but I was a little mad at Him."

As soon as I said that a collective gasp echoed through the room. With that gasp Jesus handed me a gift. Like I had swallowed a gallon of coffee I instantly had energy. I looked at them and they looked at me, unblinkingly, in shock. "Oh wait," I said. "Did you know you can tell God when you're mad at Him?"

They sat dead still except for their little heads shaking no. What followed was nothing short of holy. I told them that God desires our honesty, and He can handle our emotions. He isn't shocked when we're mad, and through it all we can trust Him. A tiny little revival broke out that week as kids were honest with God for the first time. They wrote their notes of frustration and anger and sadness to God. Everyone talked about trusting Him. It was beautiful. It was healing. It was humbling. It changed me forever. Perhaps that was the first time I truly realized the power of authenticity to point others to Jesus. I've been a different speaker and person since that moment.

Let me be authentic with you for a moment. Perhaps you caught this in the story I just shared, but I was not handling things well at the time. I was stuck in three major areas. One, I wanted to fix everything. Instead of simply listening and loving, I fell into the trap that said I was supposed to fix things. But we don't fix, my friends, we point kids to the Great Fixer.

Two, I owned too much of their stories. I let those stories seep into every part of me and I owned them. I took hurt and fear and anger on as my own. They weren't mine to own. I was called to walk with them for that moment in their journey, I was not called to own their journey.

Three, I thought I was in control. Can I get a witness? Anyone sensing a theme in my life? Control. As if the God of the universe can't do His job, I tried to control everything. Even in my brokenness I was fighting with God to let me out from under the anointing He had put on me. At one point I even asked Him to take my gifting and give it to someone else. I was so busy trying to fix and own and control that I forgot that I was merely a servant to be used, not the Master to ordain. Yikes. Tough lessons indeed. Lessons that I constantly must revisit.

AUTHENTICITY FACILITATES BEAUTY

Fast-forward four years after that moment at Lake Swan Camp and I'm at a large youth conference speaking to a packed-out room of over 800 high school students. At the end of my session a girl waited to talk to me. "Miss Mel, do you remember me?" She was vaguely familiar. "You might not remember this but four years ago at Lake Swan Camp you listened to my story. We sat at the altar, and I told you my story and we cried together. It changed everything for me. Everything was different after that. Thank you for listening."

Tears came to my eyes as she went on to tell me what God was doing in her life. Honestly, I didn't remember the details of her story, but I knew it had been a rough one. I also knew the timing meant it was the summer that God broke me. I hugged her and told her "Thank you."

We rarely get glimpses like that. I call them "glimpses of Heaven" when we get a glimpse of God's great choreography. So often we trudge forward hoping, praying we're doing something right when little do we realize God is behind the scenes choreographing pure beauty.

Authenticity facilitates beauty such as this. Honest stories, honest emotions, and honest struggles set the platform for honestly beautiful stories.

People who raise up world changers are people who are authentic. They're honest about their struggles and their fears and their doubts. They're imperfect and real. They're what the world is desperately looking for. Authentic world changers happen when we are first authentic with them. When we run toward the awkward instead of away from it. When we allow others to glimpse our souls. When they catch a glimpse of the great, perfect God we imperfectly serve.

Hey Reader: For some, authenticity comes easy. For others, it can feel really scary. A couple of things to remember: If it comes easy, be careful to not overshare. Decide ahead of time how far you will go with a story and put some boundaries on it. If you find it scary, I suggest planning it out. Write it down. What are you comfortable sharing? You don't have to share everything to be authentic. Decide ahead of time what you will share and try rehearsing it.

Make some notes on the next page:

CHAPTER SEVEN

The Importance of Story

STORIES ARE AT THE VERY HEART OF WHO WE ARE. Stories pass on history, they pass on faith, and they remind us of who we are and where we come from. If you stop and think about it, you'll notice that story permeates nearly every aspect of our lives. Stories are important.

Kids learn in the language of story, and if we are completely honest, adults learn in the same language. There is something about story that can quickly quiet a room full of kids. There is something about story that can calm a child before bed. There is something about story that is unforgettable. There is something about story that leaves an imprint. There is something about story that invites us in and calls us into adventure.

As we consider discipling world changers, we must understand how important story is in that discipleship journey.

YOUR STORY

When I started speaking at camps, perhaps one of the more challenging aspects was how early the morning chapels started. Unlike teen camps, kids get up earlier and are more energetic. When their chapel starts with loud singing and dancing at 8:30 a.m., it's all this non-morning person can do to not scowl at the hyper cherubs.

With a strategy that was born mostly out of sheer desperation and a tiny bit out of a vision God had given me, I began to do those morning chapels a little differently. I started asking the staff to share their stories with the campers. The desperation part was because it was morning. The vision part was the desire God had given me for kids to hear from people other than me. I believed it was important for them to connect with a variety of people. So I asked others to share their stories. Now I do this everywhere I go.

I call it "story" even though it is a testimony. Story is more relatable to kids and using the word "story" instead of "testimony" helps people not automatically kick into their "Christianized" word choice. I want them to share their stories of faith, not just their five-minute rehearsed testimony.

Usually, it is a challenge at first to convince the staff that kids can not only handle their stories but that they need to hear them. Through the years I have heard every legitimate excuse in the book for not sharing: "My story is too hard," or "I've had sex," or "I found my mom dead," or "I've done too much for their little ears." And every time I walk that teen or adult through their story, they see that God can use their story in the life of kids.

It usually just takes one. One brave soul to be willing to share their story in front of hundreds of little eyes. Once one does it, others are sure to follow. Over the years I've lost count of how many stories have been told. I've lost count of how many times I've humbly bowed my head grateful that God allows me to facilitate those moments. It's not lost on me that one of the most impactful things I do as a leader and speaker is to give my stage to someone else.

There is power in our stories.

It's that beautiful authenticity that comes pouring out and washes over those kids with a personal impact. My story touches those kids, and so do the stories told by their leaders.

I found Jesus at age five through a puppet at VBS. While I've had some extremely difficult moments in my life, I lived a pretty charmed life as a kid. A puppet will connect with some kids, but not all kids. When others share their stories of brokenness to wholeness it will speak to a whole other set of kids. From the veteran who shared about his tours in Iraq and his struggle with PTSD, to the stay-at-home mom who struggled with loneliness, to the eighteen-year-old counselor who shared about growing up in a series of foster homes, all their stories connected with kids. It's beautiful.

The other side of that beauty is what the sharing of their story does to the leader. It changes them, it grows them, it makes connections for them, and it reveals God's redemptive plan. Your story matters. Your story is powerful. Your story is redeemable. Your story is precious.

There is nothing you have gone through that God does not desire to redeem and create beauty out of. The enemy will lie to you and tell you your story is too much (or not enough). But he is wrong. Your story is beautiful, and your story needs to be heard. Every time we share our story, we allow God to redeem that which Satan intended for evil. Every single time we share our stories I believe God brings healing. The God we serve has never once looked at your story and thought, "I can't use that." He can and He will use your story, if you allow Him.

I firmly believe if we understood the importance of story and listening to others's stories, we would be quiet more. There is power in the telling *and* in the listening.

PRACTICALLY TELLING YOUR STORY

Kids need to hear your *stories,* not just your *story.* They need to hear about your daily walk with Jesus. They need to hear about the funny parts of your day. They need to hear about your failures, your triumphs, and your mediocre moments.

They learn in story. They are disicpled in story. If you're teaching kids, I would encourage you to never teach without inserting a piece of you into the lesson. You must share stories with them. Real and personal stories. That is where real change is made. If you teach kids and you don't share personally, you've missed out on something special. Share your stories.

AGE-APPROPRIATE

Being age-appropriate does matter. However, be careful that you aren't trying so hard to be age-appropriate that you aren't authentic or that you dumb your story down so far it loses its power.

Also, be aware that kids today are dealing with things that are way above their age on a regular basis. They need you to be real with them without wrecking them. If you have sexual abuse as a part of your story you can change your wording into, "People made poor choices and did things to me that hurt me." If you were abused and as a result of that went on to hurt yourself or others you can say, "Because I was hurt, I didn't know anything other than to hurt other people. I made poor choices and did things to other people that I shouldn't have. Sometimes I would even hurt myself." The kids that have been there or are currently in that place will understand it. The kids that aren't there will have heard enough to know it's serious but not so much that it will haunt them.

I prefer to err on the side of honesty. I'm extremely careful with the sexual side of someone's story. I don't exclude it, but I do help them frame it carefully. Other than that, nothing is off limits. Drugs, alcohol, suicide, cutting, etc. Kids are not immune to the real world. In fact, they are more than aware of what is going on and they're in desperate need of places where it's safe for them to sort through it all. Just like they need a safe place to wrestle with hard questions, they need a safe place to share their own hard stories.

Through the years there is little that hasn't been shared with kids and every bit of it has been redeemed.

- The sixty-year-old man who shared about being in prison for manslaughter. He didn't spend long talking about prison, but he did spend a long time talking about how Jesus wrote a new story for him. Two kids came to know Jesus because of his story.

- The Iraq war veteran who shared about his two tours. He started weeping in the middle of his story. I went and stood by him, and we finished his story together. Many kids (a large percentage of kids at this camp were from military families) found a safe person to talk to about their own parents's tours of duty. They also found a safe environment to talk about war.

- The young man who shared about being severely bullied in middle school. He teared up as he talked about finding his identity in Jesus. Countless kids told him their stories of being bullied.

- The young woman who shared about finding her mom passed out on the couch because she had tried to commit suicide. She talked about growing up in a difficult home and she talked about how Jesus walks with her. The line to talk to her was full of kids who had either contemplated suicide or had a parent who struggled with it.

- The man who shared about growing up in a Christian home and never fully understanding the love of Jesus. He ran and ran until he turned to Jesus and fell into his arms. Church kid after church kid lined up to talk to him about not understanding being a Christian.

On and on I could go with stories. Do you see it? Are you catching it? Story is so important. Authenticity is so important.

LISTEN TO THEIR STORIES

It's not often that kids are heard these days. Sure, they make noise, and they have questions, and they have random things to say but how often does anyone ask them what their story is? I'm speaking from experience when I tell you it's very rare.

When you share your story, it opens the door for kids to

share their stories with you. And by stories I don't just mean, "One time I went to the zoo and saw a gorilla the size of a tree."

I mean *their* story. Kids learn by watching and when they watch us share our stories it gives them permission to share their own. The good, the bad, and the ugly. I always encourage kids to share their stories with me or another adult. There is not a retreat or a camp that goes by without a lineup of kids wanting to share their stories.

Unlike adults, kids do not have their stories wrapped up in a neat little bow. The telling of their story will not be linear, it will stutter, it will circle, and it will be hard to follow. That's not the point. They simply need to be heard. Encourage them to share their story. If there is beauty when we as adults share our stories, how much more beauty is there when a child shares their story?

When I first started encouraging kids to share their stories, I had expectations. I figured their stories would be fairly simple or at least childlike. I was wrong. Oh, how I was wrong, and I've been proven wrong over and over again. Their stories are heart-wrenching, they are deep, they are ugly, and they are hard. Many a story has been told to me that has left me feeling physically battered and bruised. But it was told. There is healing in the telling. As they tell we get the holy opportunity to point them to Jesus, to show them where we see Jesus in their story. It's sacred. We also get to learn from them, grieve with them, journey with them, and laugh with them. It's sacred.

PRACTICALLY HEAR THEIR STORIES

I encourage one-on-one storytelling. It is very uncommon for me to allow a child to share their story with the group at large. There have been rare occasions and exceptions but very few. Kids tend to love drama and some of them badly want to share their story with everyone for the dramatic effect. I discourage that and encourage sharing their story with another person or in a small group.

Don't overmanage their story. Take the time they need and listen. Allow them to tell it, in all its messiness and just listen. Don't try to put it in order or make sense of it, just listen. Don't try to fix it, just listen. Don't presume, just listen. Do you sense a theme yet?

Shhh, just listen.

Yes, my friends, you are going to hear stories that by law you're going to have to report. The important thing is to listen first. You can act later. They need to be heard before they are managed. Listen and love well. Then, when it comes time to report, speak honestly with them. Walk them through it. Let them know what is going to happen and what you're going to do. You've built trust with them, don't abuse it. Keep that trust by being honest, present, and engaged.

A SPECIFIC WORD FOR PARENTS

If you haven't told your kids your story of faith, do not assume they know it. Stories are not passed down by osmosis, they are an oral tradition. You must tell your kids your story of faith. They need to know how God called you, redeemed you, and is using you. They need to hear not just the big moment where you turned to God, but the daily moments where you make the hard choices to follow Him. They also need to hear the stories of the times you didn't follow Him. Think authentically, think honestly, and share your story.

World changers understand the power of story. They understand the beauty of their own story because they've seen it in the context of God's story and other peoples's stories. They are able to see the great Storyteller at work in their lives. As they share, they allow God to redeem. We model that for them, we disciple them in that. We share openly. We allow God to redeem what we thought was lost and we continue to share about the God we walk daily with.

Hey Reader: Read Psalm 78:1-8 and watch for the importance of story. Did you see it? We tell our stories of God's goodness in our life so the next generation might know. How does an entire generation forget what God has done? The people they trust the most did not tell them. Your story matters.

1. Have you told your own children (or those kids you are closest to) your story?
2. What has God done for you lately that you can share?
3. Have you been guilty of thinking too little or too much of your story? Ask God to help you see it in a new light.

Who He is Matters

THERE IS AN IMPORTANT DISTINCTION TO MAKE WHEN we talk about making disciples. Our goal in raising up world changers is mold them into disciples of Jesus, not disciples of us. Please, oh please, hear me on this. This is a very fine, yet crucial, line that we must walk. The "who" we point them to matters greatly. If I make disciples of Jesus, they don't need me to access Him and to walk with Him. If I make disciples of me, they need me to access Jesus. And that is a slippery slope. Who He is matters.

CHAPTER EIGHT

Point Them to Jesus

I STARTED IN MINISTRY FRESH OUT OF COLLEGE. I WAS not a newbie to the world of ministry. I grew up in a pastor's family, a healthy pastor's family. We did life together and ministry together. Dad was never just the pastor; we were all involved. I went into my first full-time children's pastorate with wisdom...

... in some areas.

Perhaps my greatest mistake of all was assuming I knew what I was doing. On the outside I looked like I had it all together, on the inside I knew my head was about a foot underwater with no hope of coming up for air. While college had given me a degree in ministering to kids and teens it truly hadn't prepared me to *do* ministry with kids and teens. So I fell back on what I knew. I did what I had been taught. Not the worst thing in the world, but far from effective.

As a child in the 80s and 90s I knew children's ministry to be a place where I memorized things. A place where "sword drills" weeded out the truly committed Christians. A place where I learned Bible stories. A place where I had snacks. A place where at age five I fell in love with the church secretary's nephew, Joe, because he shared his Kool-Aid (sigh...Joe).

Again, not necessarily bad things, but most definitely lacking in purpose. For two years as a young children's pastor, I did what I knew. I taught kids things. I had them memorize and regurgitate on command. As a result, the kids in my ministry knew all the right "Sunday school" answers. It wasn't until later that I realized in teaching them the right answers I hadn't introduced them to Jesus and His desire to have a relationship with them. Unintentionally, I had elevated information over transformation.

During that time there was a stirring within me for something more. Looking back, I can clearly see it. However, at the time I was swimming below the surface without breathing.

I was working for an extremely demanding—at times abusively so—pastor who required at least sixty hours of documented work out of me every week. The children's ministry I was leading saw tremendous growth and had quadrupled in size in less than a year.

Between that, working on my master's degree, and adjusting to living in a completely new state all alone I didn't have time to pause to respond to the stirring in my heart. I had moments of greatness that most often were tied into my desire to be authentic and relational. But more often than not I led an agenda-centered ministry rather than a Jesus-centered one. I wanted measurable results I could report back to my lead pastor.

Unfortunately, those measurable results measured tangible things such as the number of kids in our ministry and the number of verses memorized and the number of Bibles given out instead of measuring the intangible things such as life change, character growth, and passion for Jesus.

Writing this now, years later, the older me has great compassion and grace for the younger me. You live and you learn and that's one of the beauties of life. Sadly, the fruit of those two years of ministry are kids who knew many of the right answers but do not know Jesus. They knew what the Bible said but they didn't know the Author.

TRANSFORMATION OVER INFORMATION

When we disciple, we must clearly understand the distinction between information and transformation. Information is vital to transformation, but in discipling word-changers information cannot be our number one goal. I have seen this happen in churches time and time again. The emphasis is put on information and knowledge over transformation.

The reality is that information is more measurable. It looks good on spreadsheets and it's easy to write down on an annual report. When those preschoolers get up to share their memory verse with "big church" it makes the whole church wipe their eyes and chuckle about "how dang cute" those kids are. At home it looks good for grandma and grandpa when your kids can easily spout off the family memory verse or pray on command. It feels good, it feels like we've accomplished something really important and really spiritual. However, there is a dark side to that.

Because we feel good, we often don't feel the need to go any further. We don't push toward true discipleship.

As mentioned earlier in this book, discipleship is messy and cannot be contained into a formula. True and healthy discipleship is a journey. It is not just a regurgitation of memorized verses, and it is not just a good feeling. It is going the extra mile to highlight transformation over information.

JUST BECAUSE IT HAS ALWAYS WORKED DOES NOT MEAN IT'S STILL WORKING

A number of years ago, I took over a midweek program at a local church. What had been working was no longer working and they wanted me to help. The program had been at its height in the 90s. A popular mid-week curriculum was still being used and neighborhood kids had flocked to the church.

Back then, kids memorized verses and sang songs and the

whole church seemed to be involved in reaching the kids of the community. However, somewhere along the way through the years, the church had forgotten to pause and take inventory of where they were and who they were serving. While it felt sudden to them, it was actually a rather subtle but remarkable shift in culture.

The makeup of the community around them had shifted. Due to a significant drug problem back in the 90s, the new kids coming to the midweek program in the early 2000s were kids with learning challenges, home stability issues, physical disabilities, and more. They were attending the same program their parents had attended but they were not the same kids as their parents.

They had behavioral issues, learning issues, and home issues. The curriculum being used was working against them instead of for them. It wasn't that they were worse kids, they were just different. They were cognitively not able to memorize large passages of scripture, they were not behaviorally able to conform to rigid rules, and they had little, if any, support from home. As a result, the church volunteers were frustrated and disillusioned and the program was dying.

The first thing I did when I stepped in was order a full stop to everything. We took a break in order to evaluate. I met with the burned-out volunteers, I talked to the kids, and I took inventory. There was no problem with the heart behind the original program, but nobody had evaluated its effectiveness in quite some time. It just wasn't effective, not anymore. And that was okay. It's okay to admit that something that used to work doesn't work anymore. It's okay to evaluate and revamp something or even put something to death. That is okay.

We took six months off and then we started back slowly. We changed to a generic curriculum where we prioritized kids experiencing the love of Jesus. Our goals switched from getting through an entire lesson each week to making sure every kid who came in the door had eaten enough food that day, got seen and affirmed by a leader, and knew they were safe and loved.

We wanted our kids to not just know about Jesus but to experience Jesus.

We wanted that church to be a place where Jesus was not

just preached but where Jesus actually came and dwelt in the neighborhood.

We wanted that place to be a place where kids had full bellies first. Full bellies help a lot with listening ears.

We wanted every kid who stepped into that program to know that they were valuable, they were seen, and they were loved.

We wanted them to know Jesus.

Honestly? It wasn't a flashy program. There were no ribbons or awards. The kids were messy and broken. We did not file them on stage for any performance. But each volunteer was changed, and every kid there knew Jesus loved them and saw them. Not flashy but beautiful.

Information without transformation rarely sticks (we'll talk more about this later). Meaning, information is important, but information should not be our first goal. Our world changers must be transformed. Webster's Dictionary defines transform as "to change in composition or structure, to change the outward form or appearance of, to change in character or condition." In order to change the world, they must first, they themselves, be transformed. Just a reminder though, we do not transform, that's the Holy Spirit's job.

Ezekiel 36:26 NLT says, *"And I will give you a new heart, and I will put a new spirit in you. I will take out your stony, stubborn heart and give you a tender, responsive heart."*

Our job is to point them to Jesus over and over again and create space for them to be transformed. Keep reading, it's about to get really good!

Hey Reader: Did you resonate with me in this chapter?

1. Have you been guilty of focusing too much on information?
2. What are some of your written or felt goals for your kids?
3. Which ones could you tweak to aim towards transformation?

CHAPTER NINE

Create Space for Them to Listen

IN *EXPERIENCING GOD* BY HENRY BLACKABY, HE teaches that "God is always at work around you." In chapter three, I reminded you that we can be assured of God's presence. He is at work, and He is present.

In John 5:17 NLT Jesus says, "My Father is always working, and so am I." He is at work around us, regardless of our age. Our job is to be on the lookout for His work and to listen for Him. As we are discipling world changers it's important for us to keep that truth at the forefront of our minds.

GOD SPEAKS TO CHILDREN

We know from the story of Samuel in 1 Samuel 3 that God has been in the business of speaking to kids since Biblical times. I love Samuel's story. God is audibly speaking and the priest, the adult, sleeps through it three times. We know from the story that God was no longer using Eli but still, GOD WAS SPEAKING OUT LOUD AND HE MISSED IT. I wonder how many times I miss God speaking. I personally believe that kids can hear God much more easily than adults. They are interruptible, they're curious, and their aching to know God has yet to be dulled by the hardness of the world.

I used to think that I needed to teach kids how to listen for God. Then I realized they are already hearing God. My job switched from teaching to creating space for them to hear from Him. We run kids so hard. They go from one activity to the next with hardly a break. If they have a break, they are on a device or music is playing or some kind of stimuli is at work. We do this both in our homes and in our children's ministries at church. If God is at work and if God is speaking but we are running at warp speed, we cannot be surprised when we can't hear Him. We must adjust.

FROM PASSIVE OBSERVERS TO ACTIVE PARTICIPANTS

When I'm teaching children, I pause in front of them before I even start my lesson. I get their attention and tell them God has something to say to them. I'll often say, "What's my job here today?" They answer, "To talk to us!" or "To preach" or "To speak." I say, "My job is to tell you what God has placed on my heart to tell you." Then I ask them what their job is. "To listen." "To sit still." "To be good."

I tell them that those are all good ideas but actually their job is to listen for God, to be on the lookout for what He wants to teach them. "God has something to say to you and your job is to prepare your heart and then to watch for God."

I always remind them that they are not there by accident. God wanted them there for this moment. They need to be on the lookout for why. This takes them from being a passive observer of the lesson to being an active participant in what God is doing. It helps their brains to engage because they now have a "job" or a purpose. This switch is incredibly important for world changers. They are not just on this earth to observe but rather to take action and be a part of what is happening. And just a reminder that when we look for God, we always find Him (Jeremiah 29:13-14).

Helping them understand my job and their job always makes them pause for a moment. Has it ever stopped you? God desires to say something to kids through your teaching, through your words, through your lessons. Whether you are in front of a group of kids in a church or you are driving the school carpool, God desires to use you. Remember, while He doesn't need you, He desires to use you, and He will. So often we get caught up in the doing and we forget that what we do is sacred. You are pointing kids to the God of the universe. That should give you pause often. Do not take this lightly.

I always explain to kids how to prepare their hearts. It's as simple as them asking God to teach them something new. I give them a quiet moment to pray and ask God to speak to them.

HOW GOD SPEAKS

Now this whole idea of God speaking can be very confusing to kids. I have seen so many adults forget that kids are literal. When we say "speak", they think they'll hear an audible voice.

I'll never forget as a young children's pastor being at a camp and listening to the speaker around the campfire. She told them God was going to speak to them, they just had to listen. As an adult I understood what she meant, as a children's pastor I was frustrated that she wasn't clearer. I was sitting by an eight-year-old boy. He did his best sitting still if I was rubbing his back. The speaker told us to bow our heads and he dutifully bowed his head and folded his hands. There was silence around the campfire as kids listened for God.

Perhaps my little guy was the only kid honest enough to admit what wasn't happening. He looked up at me after about a minute, threw his hands up in the air, and loudly proclaimed for all to hear, "I got nothing!" We must be clear with kids.

If we are going to talk to kids about hearing from God, we must explain what that means.

My favorite way to explain how you can hear God is by

asking if they've ever "heard" something from their parents without hearing their voice. This always stumps them until I break out "the look." "Oh yeah, I always know I'm in BIG trouble if my mom gives me the look!" Then they go on to talk about other ways their parents talk to them without using their voices. Hand motions, eye contact, nodding of a head, a hand squeeze, etc. Then I explain to them that God can speak to us without using His voice.

"Sometimes we might hear His voice but other times we might feel something. Have you ever been singing a song in church and felt something in your tummy? Or have you ever been reading your Bible or hearing a Bible story and suddenly noticed something new that you thought was really cool? That was God speaking to you. Sometimes you might feel something, or see something, or you might hear something. God wants to speak to you."

Notice that I use words kids understand. Kids are not going to understand that God can "speak to your heart" or "stir your soul." That just confuses them. If you are going to use "adult" language, make sure you explain it thoroughly.

When I'm done speaking or the kids are done with Sunday School or VBS or even in our home at the end of the day, I always take a minute to have them pause and think/pray about what God taught them. I reiterate what I said at the beginning and then I stay silent while they talk to God and listen for Him. I think we are too quick to move kids along without allowing them to pause and listen and respond (more on this in the next chapter).

World changers are people who know how to hear God's voice. They expect it and listen for it. That voice is what ideally will keep them grounded, growing, and teachable.

Hey Reader: Kids are already hearing from God.

1. How can you create space for them to recognize that? These do not have to be huge shifts but most likely simple tweaks.
2. In your home?
3. In your ministry?

CHAPTER TEN

Give Them Tools

I SPOKE AT MY FIRST SUMMER CAMP IN 2011.

Little did I know that first camp would spur more camps and ten-plus years later I would spend every summer at camps telling kids about Jesus. My first couple of summers I focused on what I wanted the campers to learn about Jesus at camp. I crafted my messages around what would happen at camp. After a couple of years, I changed my approach.

Reason one for this change was after a week at camp, campers went back to their "normal" lives at home. They had struggles and hardships and while camp had been a wonderful reprieve in their year, it was only one week out of the year. It did not seem to affect the rest of their lives.

The other reason was because I saw repeat campers. They were the ones who had been at the same camp the year before. They would tell me how much camp had meant to them the year before but then honestly tell me they had kind of forgotten about God for the rest of the year. I was not content with that, so I shifted. Instead of focusing on what they would learn at camp I started focusing on what they would take home from camp. That may seem like a subtle shift, but it changed everything. It gave me a long view of how and what to teach.

Whether I am teaching kids at camp, at my church, or in my home, my focus is on helping them encounter Jesus in a way that changes them forever. I'm always thinking about how to equip them to continue walking with Jesus.

MAY I BE FORGETTABLE

Going from a children's pastor to a full-time speaker, author, and coach was a major shift for me. I was used to doing life with kids and families and watching them grow.

Discipleship was living life alongside other people. I loved it. When my calling shifted, I had to think differently about how to disciple. While I thought it was specific to my unique job of speaking to a group of kids or teens for a weekend or week, I realized that as culture shifted it was not all that unique anymore. In the church setting we do not see the same kids week after week. They are hit and miss and while they may say our church is their church home, it does not guarantee that we see them very often. Who we are, who we point them to, and how we disciple them matters greatly.

Knowing I will only see kids for a short period of time has vastly adjusted my teaching. Now I focus on giving them tools for walking with Jesus when they go home, whatever that home may look like. I assume nothing because every single summer I work with thousands of kids from every background you can imagine.

While I naturally want them to connect with me, I am much more concerned with them connecting with Jesus. I am extremely intentional with the tools I give them because I am aware that, for many of them, they are headed home to a family that may not understand what Jesus is doing in them. My constant prayer is that I will be forgettable, and Jesus will be memorable. I want to raise up a generation of world changers who follow Jesus, not world changers who think Miss Mel is awesome.

I PRAY, YOU PRAY

I'm sure you've been there: a kid or student comes to you wanting prayer. Back in the day when I was unaware of how I was inadvertently making myself a conduit to God, I was always quick to pray with them. I would grab their hand and pray for their request. They were always thankful, and I was always happy to pray with them.

Once I realized the importance of them flexing their own spiritual muscles, I instated an unwritten rule in my life called "I pray, you pray." It's simple. If I pray with a child, I ask them to pray as well.

Here is why: I do not want them to think that they need Miss Mel in order to talk to God. I want them to know that God hears them when they talk to Him. While it's nice to have someone to pray with, they do not need a pastor or an adult or anyone else to approach the throne. I'm discipling world changers and world changers know they can talk to Jesus whenever they want.

It goes like this: They share what they want prayer for, and I say, "Let's pray about this. First, I'm going to pray and then I want you to pray. I want you to pray because I want you to remember that you can always talk to God whether I am here or not. He wants to talk to you." It is really as simple as that. About ninety percent of kids have no problem with this. They may be shy at first, but I do not give them a chance to say no. I will literally grab their hand and start praying out loud and when I'm done, I'll just keep my head bowed. If it's quiet for too long, I gently walk them through it.

The other ten percent will say things like, "I've never prayed out loud." Or, "I don't want to." Again, I leave them little room for argument. Sometimes I have them repeat after me or sometimes I encourage them to simply say, "Jesus, help me." Other times I'll have them whisper or pretend I'm not there and just mouth the words. Hear me on this, I have never ever had a kid not pray. Never.

I have even had kids with special needs make noises or close their eyes to indicate they are taking the initiative to talk to God. For many kids it is the first time they have prayed outside of a dinner table or have even ever prayed at all. The vast majority of the time the honesty of their prayers brings me to tears. Most often they go further with their prayers than I would expect. Once they start talking to Jesus they can't stop. The important thing is helping them connect with God personally and fostering their relationship with Him.

RESPONSE

In the previous chapter I mentioned response. This may be one of the most important things I do with kids. I create space for them to respond to what God is doing in their lives. I've already set them up by reminding them that they are there for a reason and God has something to say to them. Now I need to pause and allow them to respond.

There are a hundred ways to do this but the thing I do most often is create a response wall. All week at camp or during VBS or in our children's ministry rooms, I create space for kids to respond to what God is saying. It is one thing for them to listen for God. It's a whole other thing for them to respond to God.

Raising up world changers means we raise up kids who don't just play it safe. We want to raise up kids who act, who respond, who move forward. As they grow into adults these elements are key. Our pews are full of Christians who feel things but never do things.

Every place I go I bring string, push pins, index cards, and clothespins (I could open a laundry with all the clothespins I've accumulated over the years). It usually involves little more than putting up string on a wall and providing index cards, pens, and clothespins. I have had response stations be baskets where they can put their notes to God. I have pinned string to stage curtains, used rolling corkboards, set up buckets, etc. What these response stations look like matters little. The important thing is that there is a place for them to respond. In fact, the more normal and non-fancy the better because it helps normalize that this is something they can take home and do.

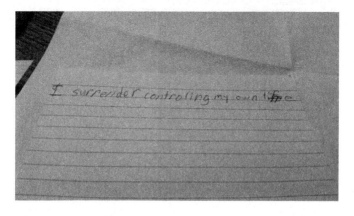

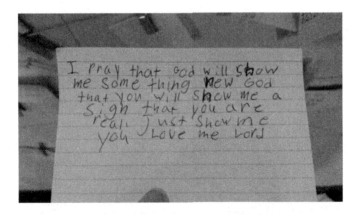

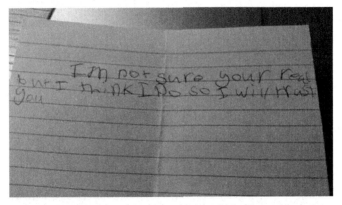

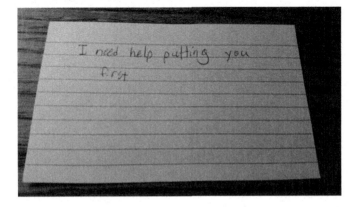

I use these response stations at the end of my lesson. I explain that it's a place for them to talk to God. They can draw a picture, scribble, or write something. God can read whatever they put on their paper, and they don't need to put their name on it because He knows them.

When they pin it to the wall (or throw it in a basket) they are symbolically giving it to God. If God has taught them something I encourage them to write it down. If God has convicted them about something I encourage them to write it down. I may give them a suggestion based on what I was teaching. For instance, if I was teaching about how "with God's help I can do hard things", I might suggest they write down something they want God's help with. More often than not, they do not need much leading.

There is something powerful in the act of them physically moving and physically writing something down and then physically giving something up. The awesome thing about kids is that this is curiously easy for them. They will come in floods to talk to God at the response stations. I have to do very little explaining. When possible, I like some quiet music playing and I remind them that this is between them and Jesus so there is to be no talking with the people around them. Most of the time I just say, "go and do business with God." I also always encourage the leaders to respond as well. Kids need to see us talking to Jesus the same way they are.

Over and over again I will remind them that it is not a magic wall or station. It's just string and push pins. It's simply a place where they can talk to God. I tell them they can take the idea home with them and create their own prayer walls. And take it home many of them do. I recently talked to a mom who told me they were upgrading their daughter's room because she was becoming a teenager. The one thing her daughter wanted to cross over into her teenage room was her prayer wall. She had put one up a few years before and she uses it regularly. She just started middle school. What a difference it will make that she has tools to equip her as she faces all that comes with middle school. She knows God, she talks to Him, she listens to Him, she is becoming a world-changer.

The next tool, God's word, needs a whole chapter.

Hey Reader: We're going to get into more tools as we move through the rest of the book.

1. What would you add here?
2. What tools have you used to help the kids you minister to and love keep walking with Jesus as they go about their lives?
3. How might you implement one of these simple ideas in the next week or month?

CHAPTER ELEVEN

Point Them to God's Word

THE BIBLE IS THE STORY OF JESUS'S LOVE AND RE-demption for us. It is the "information" for the transformation and yet it in and of itself is transformational.

Take a minute and ask yourself this question, "What in the Bible is crucial for the life of a child to know?" Focus on the word crucial. Take a minute and jot down some ideas here:

-
-
-
-
-

The key word is "crucial." We know from Hebrews 4:12 that the word of God is living and active. It is relevant, it is alive, it is powerful. Did you know that before the pandemic a regular attender only came to church twice a month? When we drill down into the math of the time we have with kids at church, it's shockingly short. Parents, you have more time with your kids, yes, but even your time is being ever limited by the pull of sports, media, friends, and more. What is crucial for these world changers to know? What is going to be a game-changer in their lives?

I cannot tell you what you should think is crucial, I can only share what's crucial for me while reserving the right to change and adjust my list as I grow and learn. My heart and methods are always pointing kids to Jesus. I want kids to fall in love with Jesus. If they fall in love with Jesus, they want to read His story. Period. When they encounter Jesus, they want to know more and to know more they go to the Bible. It's happened time and time again.

On their own they begin to dive into God's word and His story for them. What happens so beautifully is that things flip-flop. The information we held to so tightly actually comes back into play as they are transformed. Instead of highlighting information as the most important thing, we highlight transformation while introducing them to the information found in God's word. See the cycle? See the shift? Isn't that just like God to give us both?

Please keep in mind we are raising up world changers in an experiential and argumentative culture. In short, there will be many who want to argue with the Bible, about the Bible, and with those of us who believe in the Bible. This is not an apologetics book nor does it claim to be. That being said, how we explain the Bible to our kids matters. Here is how I go about it.

The Bible is history: I can tell kids that the Bible is true repeatedly but for some reason it's not until I switch to telling them it's a piece of history that it clicks in their minds. I'll often ask them to point out other historical things they know. They'll list "George Washington," "World War II," etc. I point out to them that just like World War II happened the Bible is true and it's a piece of history. It happened and it's important to know.

It's God's story: Once we establish it is history, we move on to helping them understand that it's God's story. The Bible is a part of the story God has been writing since the beginning of time. They are a part of God's story even today. So history is being written even today as they choose to follow God and enter into His story.

It's their story: God's story isn't done and if they have decided to start a relationship with Jesus, they are a part of God's story which means it's part of their story. The Bible is relevant because it applies to them today.

It's awesome: Somewhere along the way kids have decided that the Bible is boring. Unfortunately, I think adults can take most of the blame for that. Either we're not helping them enter God's story or we're not engaging them in the story. Regardless, they need to know that the Bible is incredible. You can tell them that, but the best way is to show them by inviting them into the story.

When I think about the Bible in terms of discipleship I see it as a guidebook, as a source of life, and I see it as crucial. With that being said, I have to think in terms of discipling world changers. I want kids to fall in love with Jesus and then I want them to dive into His word. When I speak to kids and teach them, I stick to crucial things that I believe will help facilitate those goals while keeping in mind I have limited time with them. I welcome you to add to this list, adjust the list, make it yours. The important thing is that we're giving them crucial truth that will help shape them.

GOD'S CHARACTER

The reality is the Bible means nothing to somebody who doesn't believe. 1 Corinthians 1:18 NLT says, *"The message of the cross is foolish to those who are headed for destruction! But we who are being saved know it is the very power of God."*

Once I establish the reality and character of God, a person's view of the Bible changes. God's character is crucial. On a side note, people can argue with the Bible and history and science and just about everything else. They cannot, and will not, argue with your own personal experience, your story. In teaching about the character of God there is never a time you should not be inserting your own story and experience into the lesson (feel free to go back and read the chapter on your story to remind yourself). It isn't just something I'm teaching, it's what I know to be true.

He is trustworthy.
He is for us.
He redeems.
He is at work around us.
He loves us.
He is always with us.

You'll notice I don't list any particular verses with these crucial characteristics of God. God's character permeates every bit of the Bible. It's less about teaching kids a specific verse and more about them seeing the character of God in everything they learn and read in the Bible. It's about them not just *knowing* this about God, it's about them *believing* these truths. When we take head knowledge and it becomes heart knowledge that changes everything in our walk with God. Information and transformation collide in a glorious "aha" moment.

GOD'S PROMISES

If God is trustworthy, if His character is true, then His promises are to be trusted. This is a classic "if, then" situation. If God is real, then I can trust Him. If God is trustworthy, then His promises are true. Teaching kids God's promises without them understanding His character is backwards. It's not necessarily bad but neither is it as effective as it could be. Once a child encounters God and begins to fall in love with Him, the promises He gives are the cherry on top of a solid ice cream sundae.

Often at camp I'll spend a night talking about *choosing to believe that what God says is true.*

It's all about them choosing to trust Him. I'll write out a couple of scripture references that are some of my favorite promises of God. At the end of the night, I invite them to come up and grab a promise for themselves. I purposely don't write out the whole verse because I want them to dig into the word to find God's promise. I love seeing them excitedly open their Bibles to find their promise. Inevitably, because God is a good God, those promises will line up with what each kid specifically needed to hear.

Summer after summer, kids come up to me and show me their little pieces of paper that they have saved. The power is not in the paper but in them having encountered God through His word.

THEOLOGY

Good theology matters. Kids are naturally inquisitive and their capacity to learn deep truth has been grossly neglected for far too long.

I would argue that much of the spiritual lack that we're seeing in our younger generations today has to do with a lack of grounded theology. They know a lot of things, but they don't know why those things matter. We did not teach them solid theology.

Many of them are disillusioned with the church and deconstructing while silently longing for the heart of Jesus. I personally grieve over the fact that many can't find the heart of Jesus in their local church.

Our world changers need solid theology.

We need to be careful that we don't feed them bite-sized pieces of a big God. We need to be careful that in our attempt to be age appropriate, we do not teach them that God is limited or small. They need to know that He is a big powerful God (omnipotent). They need to know that God is always with them (omnipresent). They need to know that God knows every little thing about them and knows everything period (omniscience). They need to know that *"Jesus is the same yesterday, today, and forever"* (Hebrews 13:8) and He does not change (immutability). They need to know that God is in charge (sovereignty). As we teach kids about the Word of God, the character of God, and the promises of God we will be teaching them theology. Do this. Do it well. Do it on purpose. Do not stray from it. This is what matters. This is what changes the world.

World changers have a deep-seated belief and trust in who God is. If they're going to change the world, they cannot go into the warzone that is our world armed with marshmallows. For too long we have given kids marshmallows to do battle in the world. They know nice stories, they know nice prayers, and they know nice verses. While those nice things are nice, they are highly ineffective when their faith is being tested. Discipling world changers means giving them truth so they go into the world armed for what the world will throw at them. Church and parents, please stop considering the one hour on a Sunday your kids are in church as a bunker in the midst of the war. Our time with kids, whether we are part of the church or parents, must not be a time of sheltering but a time of preparation. Our job is to prepare them for the battle, not hide them from it.

Lastly, God's word never returns void. His word is powerful. You may be sitting there wishing you had done things differently or even kicking yourself for not seeing this earlier. Stop it. Go back and read. If God is who He says He is, then He is to be trusted. He redeems, He restores, He calls, He rescues, He doesn't make mistakes. He also is in the business of using what we deem as mistakes. We serve a God Who has never once said "oops." Take a breath and rest assured, God is using you even now.

Hey Reader: One of the best ways to work through this chapter is to do some personal reflection.

1. What about God's character has been important for you through your life?
2. What are some of God's promises that have been especially dear to you throughout your life?
3. What do you love about God's word?

How We
Disciple Matters

HOW WE DISCIPLE REALLY DOES MATTER. WE RAISE UP a generation who know a lot of things or raise up a generation that changes the world instead of the world changing them. The how is vital. The how must be considered through the lenses of who we are and who we point to. Read through this section with those lenses on.

CHAPTER TWELVE

An Unofficial Poll

WHY IS IT SO IMPORTANT TO DISCIPLE KIDS AS WORLD changers?

Can we really make a difference?

As the church?

As parents?

As a speaker I've traveled around to many different Christian colleges to guest lecture and speak in chapel. I usually take the time to do a very unofficial poll and ask the students, "Why?" Why are you here? Why are you in a Christian college choosing to follow Jesus? I tell them that, statistically speaking, they are in the minority, they shouldn't be there. Inevitably when I ask them, "Who has a friend from church or youth group that has walked away from the Lord?" Every hand will go up.

In my book, *Missing,* I talked about millennials and how more than fifty percent of them who have grown up in the church have walked away from the church. It's a staggering statistic. It has had researchers scratching their heads and making conclusions for years now. It's heartbreaking on several different levels. While I'm not immune to the heartbreak, I would rather learn what we can and then move forward to today. What can we do to not see the same mass exodus year after year? What can we do differently?

When I guest lecture in a class, I ask students what or who made the difference for them. I'll make a big list on a white board. The answers vary. Some students are quick to name one thing while others share a story.

- Parents
- Youth leader
- One person
- "I felt like I belonged"
- Missions trip
- Community
- Friends

If you'll notice in each of their answers, there is a common theme. Do you see it? It's people. Not once in my years of asking college students this question has anyone ever said, "the curriculum" or "the color of the walls" or "the service times." It *always* comes back to people.

Parents who stood in the gap and lived their faith out loud.

A youth leader who loved well and spoke timely.

A grandparent who prayed for them and loved them well.

One significant person. For many students it was just one person. Whether it was the elderly greeter at church who knew them by name and asked them about their week and noticed when they were gone. Or their small group leader. Or a peer. Or their intentional parents who loved but didn't force. Or their grandpa who spent time with them regularly and lived out his faith in front of them. The list could go on.

COMMUNITY

Community. Community is all about people. These students I

polled felt like they belonged. They felt like they had a purpose and were a part of something. They felt like they were seen.

Recently I returned to the church I grew up in. My formative years from ages 5-11 were spent in St. Croix Falls, Wisconsin. The church there celebrated their 100-year anniversary, and they invited former pastors and their families to come for the celebration. Driving back "home" had me doing some nostalgic pondering. What had made the difference for me? It was absolutely my parents, and my grandparents' love and example, but it was more than that. That church provided a loving community where I belonged, and where I mattered.

I thought of Steve. Steve was a dad with kids of his own, but he saw me. I feel like I should disclose to you at this point that I was a challenging child, not overly easy to love. I was bossy, opinionated, and abrasive. Bless me indeed. I'll never forget one winter family retreat at a camp where Steve took me under his wing and took me up and down the tubing hill. Having fun was not easy for me as a child and Steve gave me permission to have fun. He saw me and in seeing me, he gave me a safe place to be me. He made a difference in my life. That weekend celebrating the church's anniversary I got tears in my eyes when I saw Steve. I made a point to thank him for making a difference in my life growing up.

I thought of Mike and Doreen. They were one of my best friends' parents. They had me over often to play with their daughter Sarah. They pushed me out of my very stiff comfort zone in a million different ways. They taught me to make "skinny pancakes" and gifted me with the recipe and a proper pan for my wedding. They let me make cider with them, tap maple trees with them, and experience life alongside them. They saw me for me and loved me for me. It made a difference in my life and my faith journey.

When I talk to college students who are loving Jesus and I talk to other people who are walking with Jesus, I have found that they were all discipled in some part. They had others speaking into their lives and spurring them on. Discipleship does not hinge on one person. Discipleship cannot be done in a vacuum. Discipleship is best done when the body of Christ presses into one another, regardless of age.

THE "GOD FACTOR"

Every time I ask college students the question of who influenced them, there is always a nebulous answer. I call it the "God factor." The God factor is hard to explain because it is God at work when it makes no sense whatsoever. From the kid who had no religious background but heard God speak to them at age five and tell them they were going to be a pastor (that's my dad's story). To the kid who had such an overwhelming sense of God's love for them that it changed everything (that's my friend Wesley). To the kid who felt God calling them to something more. To the kid who did not want to settle for religious ritual but wanted relationship and sought it out (that's my husband).

Do you catch the beauty of the God factor? We were created by God for relationship with Him and God is constantly drawing us to Him. He pursues us because He loves us. Regardless of all the brokenness in our world, God is still in charge.

> Isaiah 46:9-11 NLT says, *"Remember the things I have done in the past. For I alone am God! I am God, and there is none like me. Only I can tell you the future before it even happens. Everything I plan will come to pass, for I do whatever I wish. I will call a swift bird of prey from the east—a leader from a distant land to come and do my bidding. I have said what I would do, and I will do it."*

I'll remind us all one more time: God doesn't need us. He desires to use us to disciple and train up, but He doesn't need us. In fact, God will work over, under, and around us if He needs to or wants to. As a person who struggles with control and who admittedly is frequently wrong, I feel an immense amount of delight and relief that God is on the throne, and I am not. He will accomplish His will.

So take a deep breath and learn from my very unofficial poll. God is in control. The same God who grieves over those who walk away is not surprised by it. The same God who calls and speaks to kids is at work even now. The same God who called you and pulled you out of the pit is in the business of doing that even now. The God factor reminds us that we serve a re-demptive, loving God who will accomplish what He desires. With or without us.

REAL STORIES

Psalm 71:17 NLT says, *"O God, you have taught me from my earliest childhood, and I constantly tell others about the wonderful things you do."*

I asked for young adults to share their stories with me. I asked them why they're following Jesus. I was flooded with emails, Facebook messages, and texts. Read through these and draw your own conclusions.

Being a Christian was a part of my family. It was a part of my "normal." I grew up in the church, I went to youth group, I attended youth events and retreats, but in total honesty, I don't remember the first time I accepted Christ. I was just four years old. However, I do remember the next time I accepted Christ...and the next...and the next. I had this weird misconception that God had just given up and left me every time I messed up, every time I sinned. I always felt I needed to keep asking Him back into my life, just to be safe. I am not sure I really understood what accepting God into my life truly entailed until my senior year. By then, I was broken completely. I was ashamed, I was sickened with guilt, and I was burdened with sin. I was a master at apologizing, but a beginner at repenting. I remember the day and place when I confessed and repented aloud all I had done. In the moment I expected to be most ashamed, turned out to be the moment I was most at peace. It was then I realized the God I asked the first time to come into my life had always been there; He had never left me. He was waiting patiently and anxiously with arms open wide waiting for me to fall into them. I had experienced the mighty grace and love of God. So why do I choose to follow Christ? See, because of Him, I am forgiven. Because of Him, I am free. Because of Him, I am made new. I am proud to be a

Christian, but I am humbled to be a Christ Follower. I am a Christian, because without Him, I am nothing.

Nicola, 19.

Hello, my name is Christopher, and I am 25 years old. I grew up in a Christian home and was raised to follow Christ and give him everything that I had. I always believed that there was a God who loved me, and I knew that I loved him. When I was 13 years old, I went to a Christian camp and felt his presence for the first time. I was going through a rough time after losing my Grandma, who was my best friend, but the speaker that week preached about something that opened my eyes. He was preaching on Romans 8:28, which says that God works for the good for those who love him and have been called according to his purpose. Now I knew that I loved God and since I knew that, I knew that he was going to turn my Grandma's death into something good. This was the first thing that woke my heart and made me chase after God. The second big thing was when I surrounded myself with a strong Christian community. I met my two best friends, Josh and Courtney, who showed me what it felt like to be loved by God's love. I really think that God used them to love on me. They also taught me how important it is to have community and to be open and honest about everything. In addition to community, they also taught me how important it is to have accountability partners, and for people to hold you account-able to spending time with Jesus, and making sure you're setting an example on how a Christian should act. My life has been a long journey and I am still learning, but these are the main two things that have made me follow God and just chase after him.

Chris, 25.

My name is Ashley. I am 21 years old and a college senior. One of the reasons that I chose my school is because it was a Christian institution but it is not my school that I largely credit my current status as a Christ-follower to.

I grew up in a very small town, with a very small church. In the summer we had a booming 75 members in the congregation, and in the winter we dwindled to about half that number. I attended this church with my grandmother. My parents would dutifully drop me off every Sunday, and pick me up when it was over. They were believers but did not raise my sister and I in the church, so I do not think they were the primary influencers in my relationship with Christ either. It was the Church that led me to Christ.

When I was eight years old, my father was disabled in an accident. His disability caused severe chronic pain and in desperation, he turned to alcohol to soothe that pain. The home became scary, and quickly. My parents would fight. My sister would cry. My dad would pick me up from school drunk, and drive me home, swerving through side streets to avoid passing the CHP station just two blocks from our house. I carried a lot of resentment in those days.

My resentment was toward my family for putting me in this situation. My resentment was toward God for putting my family in this situation. My resentment was toward the Church for not fixing the problem. Still, it was a very small town, and there was nothing else to do. I was a scared pre-teen, looking for a place to go that was not home. And Church was always open.

I became that little church's most avid little attender. I went to church on Sundays. I went to church on Wednesdays. I started volunteering with the younger kids on Tuesdays. I went to the church board meetings on Fridays. I went to prayer groups on Saturdays. If my parents weren't willing to drive me, I called one of the elderly members to pick me up (Did I mention I am the youngest member of the congregation by about 50 years?). I did not turn to the church for spiritual reasons. I was lonely and scared. I wasn't seeking God, but I was seeking a place to belong. I became the "honorary granddaughter" to about 15 different couples. The church was familiar with my home life, as my father's mother was in attendance, but no one ever asked me about it. They opened their homes to me. They welcomed me at their dinner tables.

They taught me how to knit, and plant flowers and bake the best gingerbread on the planet. In the church, I found a family who filled every hole my own broken family had left.

I had not turned to the church to find God, but the family I did find there thrust Him before my very eyes. I discovered Him and His love so fully through the families that had welcomed me. No one ever questioned why I was there. They simply used their time to show me the wonder that is a life in Christ. They taught me to release my resentment and cling to His love. I was blessed. When I came to Christ, I came to Him with the wisdom of my elders and the wonder of a child's faith.

So when I credit my faith to the "Church," I mean the body of people and not the building. It was not Sunday school or sermons. It wasn't doctrines or Bible studies. It was simply a group of adults who were so overflowing with God's love that they had more than enough to share with a scared little girl. That church is the church that saved me.

Ashley, 21.

A lot of specific, crazy yet amazing things happened to me the summer of 2016. I've grown much closer to Christ than ever before. I could explain but it'd be too much. So in short, let's just say it was my spiritual walk with God, family, relationships, college, and some other things too, but those were the main ones. I'm following Christ now because I am in love with God. I know I need Him in my life every second of every day. Through the storm and sunshine, He is with me and before me in every step of the way even when I can't see or feel Him. My relationship with Christ has gone through many ups and downs. Like the hymn ("Come, Thou Fount of Every Blessing") we sing, I'm "prone to wander" and "prone to leave" Him, but God is relentless and no matter what, I always return to Him because I just can't get over Him. His loving arms are always wide open. Without following Christ, I wouldn't be who I am today. I'd be so lost and broken. Life is tough and if I hadn't known Christ, I probably would have committed suicide or ran away or something long ago. It's not easy following Christ. There's a lot that one has to go through and sacrifice but I've learned that what I receive is more than what I give. It's hard but so rewarding at the end.

Nkaoyoua (AKA Green), 18.

I did not have a wonderful home life, so I started going to church originally just to get out of the house. I ended up joining anything I could that would keep me busy, and more importantly, gone. At first, I didn't go so that I could grow closer to God, but along the way that is what happened. I was learning verses through Bible quizzes and AWANA, I was singing songs about how amazing this God is, and I was receiving love and attention from the people at church that I wasn't getting from home. It was during this time that God got a hold of me, and although I still wasn't clear on all the details, I knew that God was the real deal and I was not going to make it through my life at home without His help.

Jennie, 24.

The difference that happened in my life is named Heidi. I am almost sure that Heidi has no idea how much of a difference she actually made in my life and she probably doesn't even remember who I am. She was my camp counselor at Camp Centrifuge when I was 15 years old. I went to camp scared, broken and confused. I had never been to camp nor did I grow up in the church, and my family had fallen apart a month before when my dad went to prison. Since I didn't know any of the topics or questions that we discussed, I would shy away to the back of the group when we would discuss anything biblical. Midweek, I had a breakdown and the emotional floodgates opened. Through tears I told her all the things that I had been holding in for a month. She sat there and allowed me to let out everything that I needed to say. She didn't run away from being overwhelmed, but instead she shared Jesus with me. She told me that I had worth and that I mattered. She told me that she loved me.

Heidi was faithful to her calling to plant seeds that summer. She pulled me from the fringes into the middle and loved me as she loved herself. Heidi was the first person to ever share the Gospel with me and she was the first person to tell me that they loved me. She absolutely revolutionized my life. Ever since then I have been passionate about following Christ and His calling for my life, sharing Him with children and young adults like Heidi did for me!

Christina (Tuna), 23.

I am following Jesus today because He is the only way. I would be completely lost without Him. Following Him is the best way to live. He has taken me on the adventure of a lifetime and I am in love with Him. I don't even deserve to be in His presence, yet He still takes me in, day after day, sin after sin. I am following Him now because of the people who took me in during the most broken moments of my life. I was not coerced or pushed into following Jesus, I was taught, discipled and mentored by older students and leaders at my local church.

Carlos, 21.

Bringing someone to Christ, leading someone in deep pain to God's healing, and seeing what happens firsthand:

This has been one of the most influential moments in my life, to see someone in pain and know there was nothing I could say or do to make this better. So I asked God what to do and He showed up. I didn't say everything just right, but I knew God's love was being shown and it wasn't about me anyway. God made His presence known and I got to see a person held down by past mistakes find freedom because she heard God's offer and accepted it. I thank God every time I remember this moment for the gift of letting me be there.

Leaders in the church influencing my faith:

My middle-school years were formative in my faith. I was in a lot of pain and was living a life of fear and nothing was making me feel better. So I asked the people that I looked up to (the pastors and youth leaders of my youth group) what they do when this happens. They told me to go to God's word, that when we hear lies and believe them, the best thing to do is to go to the truth. So I did. It didn't immediately "work" like I thought it would, I didn't know at the time that I was forming a stronger bond with the God of the universe, I was just continuing to have conversations with those leaders and listen to their advice. Then when something difficult happened (like being bullied in school) it wasn't this terrible life-altering pain like it used to be. The situation was the same, but I was different. There was no way I was going back to the same way of life ever again. I'm following Christ now because the people that consistently took an interest in my life always pointed to God. He was always using creative ways to tell me just how much He loves me, just like they said He would.

Being a disciple:

When I was in eighth grade, myself and one other student were given responsibilities and opportunities to teach/lead. We looked at each other wide-eyed and afraid, both thinking "These people are crazy, we can't do this!" And then we did. We were given more responsibility and sometimes said things wrong and fought with each other, but we had those same leaders always praying with us, gently correcting us, and teaching us how to do this thing we thought we couldn't do. When given the opportunities to have faith, we asked God for faith. God showed up and we did. I was told I could be a disciple and that I had the same God guiding and teaching me as the other great leaders of the faith.

Amanda, 21.

Why am I following Christ now? That's a great question that's not often thought about. I grew up in a Christian home and that's all I would see around me. One gets very used to it and I became very comfortable with it, then I remember getting saved when I was about 9 years old. When growing up in the church it's VERY easy to think your testimony isn't good enough cause you can't recall that drastic before and after experience. But it wasn't till I was about 18 that I really started believing in God for real. I had believed it all along, but it had never felt so real. It had reached a point where I felt distant from God all the time and it felt so normal, I hated it. My attitude was changing, depression kicked in, college started, many life decisions. It was a lot at once but I felt like I knew I needed to go through that in order to have that genuine relationship with Christ. I still struggle with having that "ideal" relationship but it still works for me. God is the reason we're living and there's nothing else that makes sense to me about how the world came about besides that.

Alex, 20

Hey Reader: Do some reflecting.

1. Why are you here?
2. Who or what has made a difference in your life?
3. Why do you care about raising up world changers?

CHAPTER THIRTEEN

Intentionality

"INTENTIONALITY" IS A KEY WORD WHEN WE ARE DIS-cipling world changers. Being intentional means we do things on purpose. Regardless of our intentions, we will inevitably leave an imprint on the kids we encounter. I recently heard a wise older woman say, "If you're working with kids, you're leading them." So true. The very way God designed kids and their developing brains means we are impacting them, leading them, and leaving an imprint on them. Being intentional makes the difference in the type of impact we make.

BUILD TRUST

Kids today will not respect you simply because you are an adult. Those days are gone. "Because I said so" or "because I'm in charge" are no longer workable qualifying statements for a kid's question of "Why do I have to?" This whole slide away from respect of authority figures is not just a problem in the United States of America. This is a worldwide reality. I talk to leaders and parents around the world who are aware of this. We can stop here and complain and be frustrated or we can see that these kids are asking for something more. They want to know us.

What they're saying to us is this, "I don't respect you until I trust you and I don't trust you until I know you."

I've tested this theory out for years. I've taught it to school-teachers, parents, and children's ministry leaders and each time it has proven to be true. Kids today are hungry to know us. They want to be able to trust us. In their own little skeptical way they are asking for us to prove that we are worth listening to.

Building trust with kids, much like many other things, is much less formulaic and much more relational. It's intention-ally allowing them to get to know us. It's being authentic and open with them. It's allowing them to enter into our world.

For some of you this is a very easy process because you are naturally open. For others this is going to be more challenging. It is, however, necessary to build trust with kids. Once you have their trust, you've earned "the right" to disciple them. You've earned "the right" to be heard by them.

There are several ways you can earn kids's trust. I have a couple of things I do. Keep in mind, when I speak at camp or retreat, I have a very limited time period to earn their trust. If I don't capture their trust in the first ten minutes of speaking to them, I will most likely never capture it. Through the years I've learned that the best way for them to get to know me is to allow them to ask me questions. Before I ever jump into my lesson, I allow them ask me anything they want and I promise to answer it. As they ask and I answer, they get to know me.

I also do Two Truths and a Lie with them. I typically start with this because it gives us a foundation to work from. There is something about this game that kids love. They LOVE it. I don't quickly think of things for this game, so I write them out ahead of time. I give them three facts about me, one being a lie, and they must vote on what they think the lie is. I always preface this by telling them I will never lie to them except for when we're playing the game. I work hard to find things that are fascinating or will lead to a good story to tell them. Such as:

1. I've eaten ox tongue in Hong Kong.
2. I rode a camel in Africa.
3. I was chased by a donkey in Mexico.

Once they vote, I tell them what the lie was (#2) and then they inevitably want to know the story about me being chased by a donkey. By the time I'm done with that story, they've gotten to know a little about me and they have begun to trust me. I've earned their respect.

Take a minute and jot down a few ideas for Two Truths and a Lie.

-
-
-
-
-
-

EXPLAIN

"Why?"

How many times have you heard that question come out of a child's mouth? Some of you parents go to sleep at night with that word resonating in your heads. Kids are naturally inquisitive and designed by God to learn. We must keep in mind that one of the ways they learn is by asking questions. While I certainly don't encourage answering every single "why" question, I do encourage you to do a little preemptive work with kids. Explain things ahead of time.

As adults, we naturally do things that we've learned through the years. For us it has become routine or tradition. We rarely think of why we do certain things. For a child those things are all new. They'll learn the routine and the tradition, but it takes on greater meaning when they understand the "why" behind it.

For instance, when we pray, we bow our heads, fold our

hands, and close our eyes. Why? This isn't a bad thing but why do we do it? Kids have no idea. Honestly, someone new to church or even someone watching you pray in a restaurant could very likely not understand why you do that.

I always explain it to kids. I take a moment to intentionally explain to them why we do certain things.

"When we pray, we bow our heads. God can hear us if our heads are up but when we keep them down it's easier to stay focused on God. We close our eyes. God can hear us if our eyes are open but when we close our eyes we stay focused on Him. We fold our hands. God can hear us if our hands aren't folded but it helps us to keep our hands to ourselves and not interrupt someone else who is trying to stay focused."

It's about giving them context and helping them understand why we do certain things.

Once I've clearly explained how we pray, I'll do things to further emphasize that God can hear us no matter what. We'll pray with our eyes open (kids love this), we'll pray with our hands waving in the air, we'll pray while jumping, etc. I want them to understand they can pray anytime. The how is not nearly as important as the heart.

Take a moment to think through how often you do or say things that could be explained to kids. Explaining gives us the opportunity to beautifully weave together the context and story behind why we do or say things. From big Christian words to practices of faith, to age-old Bible stories, intentionally explain the "why" behind it all. It will open doors for discipleship that you would never have imagined.

Jot down a few things that you do that you should explain:

-
-
-
-
-
-

MODEL

Kids learn by watching us. They are extremely observant. They take their cues from us. How we react to hard things, how we love people, how we pray, how we apologize, how we persevere, and so much more, deeply impacts them. We must intentionally model for them what walking with Jesus looks like.

I was on stage at Camp Rivercrest in Fremont, Nebraska. Two-hundred pairs of eyes were watching me. We were laughing together, sharing stories, and having a grand ol' time. One kid in particular in the front row had a quick wit.

He could take what this sarcastic, quick-witted speaker could dish out and I loved it. I don't remember what he said but I do remember that my response to him crossed a line. What I meant to be funny passed into mean. He laughed good-naturedly, but I was convicted. I kept talking with the kids while the Holy Spirit was convicting my heart. I hadn't led well. I was embarrassed and ashamed. I knew I needed to apologize to him but honestly, I didn't want the adults in the room to see me "lose face."

I finally got over myself and stopped. In front of everyone I said, "I need to apologize to you. I was trying to be funny but instead of being funny I was mean. It was not okay, and I am sorry. Will you forgive me?" The little guy was embarrassed and gracious. "Miss Mel, it's okay, you didn't hurt my feelings."

"I crossed a line, and I shouldn't have done that. Will you forgive me for using my words to put you down instead of building you up?"

Of course, he said yes, and we moved on. I was shaking in my flip-flops after that encounter. Talk about being stripped bare and having all my dirty laundry hang out. Awkward! The pastor in me, the adult in me hadn't liked that whole encounter in the least. Then I realized what a powerful moment that had been. I had modeled humility, I had modeled apologizing, I had modeled the value of that kid, I had modeled that not all adults have it all together all the time. It had been powerful.

I still cringe when I think of that moment and yet I learned a powerful lesson in modeling what walking with Jesus looks like. It means I do humble myself. It means I admit when I'm wrong. It means I will feel uncomfortable at times but it's worth it. Intentionally modeling what walking with Jesus looks like means I purposely enter into the hard moments, so they see I'm a real imperfect adult serving a real perfect God.

Modeling takes all sorts of forms. It can look like looking someone in the eye when they're talking. Taking a moment from busy work to dance with your five-year-old in the kitchen. Laughing when something goes wrong instead of being angry. Choosing to pray first before worry sets in. Showing kindness to someone who hasn't been kind to you. Greeting everyone like they have value, because they do. Giving food to someone in need, smiling at a cranky person, crying when you're sad, rejoicing when you're happy. And on and on it goes.

It is, however, intentional. It's purposefully allowing our kids to see us walking with Jesus through each circumstance. And catch this, how we react when we model a behavior we regret will often speak louder than if we had done the right thing.

In what areas can you model for the kids you encounter?

-

-

-

-

-

-

SPUR THEM ON

God created kids for adventure. Part of their growth and development is tied up in their reach for hard things, trying what seems impossible, and pushing past what they thought they could do. This is less about their physical activity and more about their spiritual activity.

For far too long we've set the bar too low for our kids. As I alluded to earlier, in our desire to bring things to their level we've dumbed-down the Christian walk. We've given them a neat and tidy Jesus. It's been too easy. No wonder they get bored and walk away. No wonder they look for adventure elsewhere. No wonder. Just like adults, kids do their learning in the nitty-gritty. It's what shapes them and defines them.

I urge you to spur them on. To push them to dig deeper, to encourage them to look for themselves, to be their biggest cheerleader as their life gets hard. Spur them on. This theme has been throughout this book, so I won't park here long but please, oh please, hear me on this: Don't allow them to settle for a safe existence. Don't rush to fix it, rather spur them on to figure it out for themselves.

When I was learning to ride a bicycle, we were living in Wisconsin in a house with a long driveway. At the end of the driveway was a bunch of trees. I was learning to ride my bike in the heat of the summer, but my dad always made me wear long sleeves and long pants.

He knew something I didn't; he knew I was going to fall. I grumbled as sweat trickled down my back. I knew something my dad didn't know; I was invincible. Day after day it was proven that my dad was much wiser than I. Those trees at the end of the driveway were my nemesis. Day after day I couldn't make the turn and day after day I ran headlong into those trees. Day after day I ended up rolling in the dirt.

My dad was always there to pick me up, give me a hug, and put me back on the bike. He never once let me quit and he never once cut down the trees for me. He spurred me on. He gave me advice, he encouraged me, and then he watched me fail time and time again. Eventually I figured out that tricky turn. The day I made the turn without colliding into a tree was a celebratory day indeed.

Intentionally discipling world changers means we spur them on to bigger, deeper, greater things than even they think they can do. It's about preparing them and it's about letting them go. It's about being there no matter what the outcome. It's about celebrating the victories. It's intentional.

Living intentionally means we do things on purpose. We don't claim perfection, but we do claim purpose. It's what sets us apart as Christ-followers. We intentionally chose Jesus over and over and over again.

Hey Reader: Go back through the chapter and write down your three best ideas for being intentional below:

1.

2.

3.

CHAPTER FOURTEEN

Choices

I TOUCHED ON THE IMPORTANCE OF KIDS'S CHOICES IN my first book, but I want to expand on it even further here. In order to change the world, our world changers are going to need to operate differently than the world. They are going to have to make tough choices that are countercultural. Whether they are aware of it or not, their choices will define their lives. In a culture where it is not only permissible, but acceptable, to rarely take responsibilities for our own actions this is a crucial area for discipleship. It's not enough to know, that knowledge must translate into action. Kids must be taught the impact of their choices.

We're by nature very selfish people. While as adults we know our choices affect others, we don't often remember that fact in the individual moments. When we send a quick text while driving, gossip behind a friend's back, under-tip a server, etc. Do we often stop to realize how our choices always affect more than just ourselves?

DAVID

I believe the area of choice is imperative for kids to learn. They need to understand that they can make their own choices and that their choices impact others. One of my favorite stories in the Bible about choice is David and Goliath. I love to take the kids through that story and show them all of the choices that affected the story. We repeat over and over again, "My choices always affect me and the people around me." In the case of David, his choices on that day when he went to visit his brothers changed the course of history. We don't always know the full impact of our choices but there is always an impact.

1 Samuel 17:17-19: David chooses to obey his dad. His dad asked him to go check on his brothers and take them some food. I don't know David's feelings in that moment, but he chose to obey his dad. He agreed to go bring cheese (v.18) to his brothers. He set off, I guarantee, not knowing he was going to determine the entire future of the Israelite people.

1 Samuel 17:20: David leaves his sheep with another shepherd. This shepherd has no name and yet his choices are crucial to this story. His chose to watch David's sheep. He could have said no, he could have said he didn't like David's sheep, instead he agreed to watch the sheep so David could go on his way. I'm quite sure he wasn't watching his extra helping of sheep that day thinking to himself, "Man, today my choices are going to change the world." And yet they did.

1 Samuel 17:26: David is the first one in the whole story to choose to ask questions instead of choosing fear. He is the first one who remembers that the Israelites are God's chosen people and that Goliath is defying Him. Those two choices alone start an incredible trajectory.

1 Samuel 17:29-31: David chooses to walk away from a guaranteed fight that his brother was trying to taunt him into. He chose to answer the stirring in his heart and pursue the great story God had for him.

The story goes on and on and it's incredible, and it's not just because it's David and Goliath. When you begin to look at the Bible and your life through the lens of choices you begin to realize just how often your choices affect your story and others's stories.

POWER HUNGRY

Kids love having power. I just spent a couple of weeks with two of my nieces. My two-year-old niece is spot on in her development stage where she is asking the question, "Can I do it?" Yes, my friends, yes, she can do it. Even at age two that girl wants control. She wants to do things on her own. I'm quite positive an entire year went by in one day while I waited for her to crawl into her carseat and buckle herself. My five-year-old niece ran every moment of my day for me. "I have an idea Auntie Mo, how about you sit there and be really quiet and you'll get a surprise!" Kids like to have control. It is entirely appropriate to give them control in their relationship with God.

When I present the gospel to kids, I don't sugarcoat it in the least. I am completely honest about the decision it is. It is their decision alone. I explain the gospel story and I tell them that because God didn't create them to be robots but instead gave them the ability to choose for themselves, it is their decision what they do with Jesus. I share personally about my own decision to follow Jesus. I am brutally honest about how hard it is at times to follow Jesus but how I wouldn't change it for the world. I point them to scripture and then I let them decide. I don't belabor the moment. I'm honest and I let them decide. A choice that a kid makes on their own seems to "stick" more than a choice they make because someone told them to.

Look at this little girl. This first picture is day one of camp.

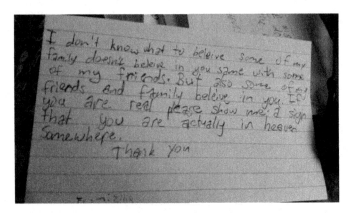

This second picture is toward the end of camp:

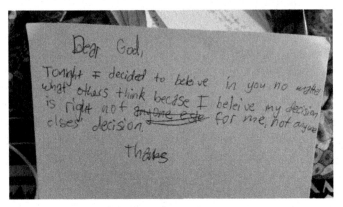

How much do you love this? She agonized over her decision. She weighed the pros and cons and made the decision she knew God was calling her to make. She made a decision that she knew wouldn't be popular with everyone in her life but she made the choice to choose Jesus. I'm quite sure she won't turn back from a decision such as this.

CHOOSING CREATES OWNERSHIP

When we allow kids to make their own choices in their relationship with Jesus, they take ownership and they embrace it. And while allowing them ownership may not always translate to the decisions we want for them in the timeline we want, there is beauty in their wrestling and choosing. And if our faith rests in a good, sovereign God, we look to Him to speak to our children's hearts. We can trust a God who relentlessly pursues His people.

My four-year-old niece called to tell me something. "Auntie Mo, I'm not ready to ask Jesus into my heart. I don't want to give Him full control of my heart." Her honesty and her reasoning had my mouth hanging open and my shoulders shaking in laughter. I told her, "Lovebug, I'm so proud of you for thinking about this. God has big plans for you, I can't wait to hear about when you are ready to give Him your whole heart." Of course, the auntie in me would have loved for that call to give a different announcement, yet the discipler in me was so proud that she was thinking for herself.

At Easter almost a year later she called me again. "Auntie Mo! I asked Jesus into my heart today! Now I'm going to Heaven with you!" I cried all the tears and told her how proud I was of her. I absolutely love that she wrestled with her decision and was finally ready to give God her full heart. She has a beautiful sweetness and sensitivity to the Holy Spirit. Just a couple of weeks ago she asked everyone in her car to, "Quiet down. I need a little Jesus time." A few days after that she told me she had found her shoes after she asked God to guide her hands. She was so excited! She prays out loud, often. She takes every little thing to Jesus and her walk with Jesus challenges me regularly. She loves her Jesus and knows He loves her.

Our job is to give kids the facts, the knowledge, the heart, and then let them decide. Another phrase I repeat with kids is, "He sees you, He knows you, He loves you. You decide." If I'm doing my job well as I disciple them, they know that God sees them, that He knows them, and that He loves them. What happens next is up to them.

Keep in mind there is beauty in the wrestling, there is beauty in the thinking, and there is even beauty in the mistakes. Those are the times that firm our foundation and season our faith. If our kids are going to be world changers, they are going to need to have a little seasoning of their faith. We're preparing them for a world that will fight back and tell them they're wrong over and over again. The wrestling and the grappling is where their strength is built. From our vantage point it's very difficult to watch at times yet it is necessary. Hold your kids with open hands and allow them to choose.

WE LOVE THEM NO MATTER WHAT

Several years ago one of "my kids" got pregnant. She was very young, and it was a tough situation. I was heartbroken for her.

One of my other kids texted me to say, "Don't worry Miss Mel, I'm still hanging on." She wanted me to know she was making good choices and was being careful. I text her back rather forcefully saying, "No matter what I love you. Always and always I love you. No choice you make will stop me from loving you and will stop God from loving you. I'm glad you're not pregnant but if you are at some point, know you can talk to me."

Please hear me on this. One of the reasons some people who grew up in the church have not gone back to church is because they are embarrassed and scared. They were taught a God of judgment instead of a God of love. God is both, but for too long we focused on judgment and not enough on His love and grace. In the midst of kids making their own choices we must show them the love of Christ through our response to their choices, good and bad.

I was in Seattle earlier this year and I met up with one of my sweet nineteen-year-old girls. She and I have been a part of each other's stories for a long time. I met up with her and had the chance to meet her live-in boyfriend. We walked up a street in Seattle and stopped to get bubble tea.

I bought them both tea and we sat down at a booth. I don't beat around the bush, so I went for it, "Tell me about this whole living together thing."

They sheepishly looked at each other and she said, "I knew you would ask." She knew I would ask because I always ask the tough questions. They proceeded to tell me how living together was going, about their cat, about their apartment. I asked them to tell me why they love each other.

Their list was adorable and we laughed together. I got serious and looked them both in the eye. "I love both of you. I am for you individually and together. You know living together is not a great choice and I wish you were choosing to do something different, but I am for you. I am praying for you, I am cheering you on, and I am always ready to talk. God loves you guys and is ready anytime for you to start talking to Him again."

My girl looked at me with tears in her eyes and her boyfriend stared at me in shock. She whispered, "Nobody has ever said that. Everyone has been mad and told us how wrong we are. Nobody has told us they love us and are praying for us." Her boyfriend got up, hugged me, and said, "Thank you."

Can I be honest? That wasn't exactly the easiest thing for me to do. I am not a fan of them living together. I'm not a fan of her choices. Recently she called me because they were breaking up and the aftermath was incredibly messy. I could see it coming from a mile away. I was more concerned with showing love and grace than I was with condemning and guilting. I listened, I cried with her, I gave wisdom, and I pointed her to Jesus.

Our world changers need to be shown the love and grace of God because they will never ever be perfect every time they make a choice. Never. And neither will you or I. Our world changers need to understand that their choices have impact, they need to be released to make their own choices, and they need to be embraced and loved regardless of their choices.

Hey Reader: It can be so hard to release control and allow those we love make their own choices. It is exactly what God did when He gave us free will. He loves us knowing we are going to make poor choices. He never gives up on us. Take a minute with your hands open in front of you surrendering those who were never yours in the first place.

CHAPTER FIFTEEN

Core Truths

IMAGINE WITH ME FOR A MOMENT, IMAGINE THAT WE are suddenly living in a world that constantly turns its back on the Creator. Imagine that we live in a world where sin and fear and doubt shout loudly, a world where a still small voice can barely be heard. Imagine we live in a world where church is not routine nor expected but rather is an afterthought. Imagine we live in a world where sports and dance and music activities pull parents and kids in one thousand different directions. Imagine we live in a world where parents want their kids to love Jesus and ministry leaders want their kids to love Jesus yet it seems everything around them screams the opposite of Jesus. Imagine.

Obviously, you didn't have to use too much of your imagination for that picture. We are living in that world today. Our world is noisy and lost and messy, but we serve a God who is none of those things. We serve a God who is steady and aware and at work. The God we serve is the same yesterday, today, and forever. He hasn't changed and His message is the same. Our environment has changed which means we have to re-think how we're communicating His message.

Ask yourself this question: If you could give your kids only three to five truths about who God is that would seep deep into their souls and become cemented in the foundation they build on for the rest of their lives, what would those truths be? Take our world into account. We need to be aware of the world our kids are living in. We cannot have a rose-colored glasses view of the world. In light of this world, in light of a good and steadfast God, what truths would you cement into the heart of your kids?

-
-
-
-

That question isn't something that can or should be an-swered quickly. I've been working on my own list for years and I'm constantly tweaking it. I've been extremely hesitant to put my own list into this book for a number of reasons. I do not want you as the reader to copy my list and adopt it as your own. I want you to wrestle through this process. I want you to scrib-ble, erase, write, and repeat. I want you to spend time seek-ing God's heart on the matter for your kids. I am also realistic enough to know that this is a fluid process and it's quite likely that by the time this book is published, I will have once again tweaked my list.

Ministry leaders, hear me on this. The list you create is what you use to drive your curriculum and your volunteers. Your curriculum doesn't tell you what is important, you tell your curriculum what is important.

Parents, the list you create are the truths you drive home every single day to your kids. They are phrases that your kids know backwards and forwards. They ground you and they guide you. They are truths that you yourself believe and live out.

MY ORIGINAL LIST

I think I first started my list in 2005. I came into a children's ministry following an effective children's pastor. I was stunned at how the beliefs of the previous children's pastor had become a part of the kids in her ministry. She was passionate about missions and the kids in her ministry were passionate about missions. She was a prayer warrior and the kids in her ministry were passionate about prayer. Perhaps it was that realization where I first truly felt the weight of my calling on my shoulders. I was going to have a chance to help shape kids.

Whoa.

I spent considerable time praying through what I wanted my legacy to be on those kids. The reality is we always leave an imprint on kids. They truly are like wet cement. Either we're intentional and leave a lasting beautiful image or we're clumsy and unaware and leave a big ugly boot print. Either way, we leave something behind. I wanted my imprint to serve them well.

My first list looked a little something like this. It had more to do with the structure of our group than it did with truth about who God is.

Prayer: We believe in the power of prayer. We will stop and pray when needed. We will pray together, and out loud, and often. No prayer request is too small. We will not be ashamed to lay hands on others and pray for them.

We were prayer warriors. We prayed often. It was not unusual for us to gather around someone, lay hands on them, and pray for them. Prayer was a part of my heart I wanted my kids to know. The fruit of that is kids today who know how to pray and are not ashamed to pray. They might not have a perfect walk with Jesus (or even much of any walk) but they pray.

Team: We are a team. Everyone belongs here. We work together, we do not single anyone out or leave anyone out. We are family.

Our 4th-6th grade youth group was called Wyldride. We went over the reason for that name with the kids on a regular basis. "Life is a wild ride. It twists and turns and it's crazy. God loves you and is always with you on the crazy ride. In the midst of the crazy this is a place where you belong. You might not feel safe at home or at school but you are safe here. We love you and we're on the ride with you."

My kids who were in that group still talk about the amount of team building I made them do. They both loved and hated it. We spent hours doing team building exercises. That age in particular is so competitive. I hated watching them compete against each other and end up fighting and angry. For one whole year I banned any type of competitive game. They spent hours on a log arranging themselves in birth order without being allowed to speak or step off the log. They did trust walks, trust falls, and anything else I could think of that would build trust. They complained and yet they still talk about how much they loved it. More than once we'd all fall off the log and end up laying in the dirt laughing until we cried. Then I'd make them get back up and start all over again. We'd spend a half hour doing team-building and the next hour was spent in small groups and worship and time with Jesus.

One year in particular my older kids were beginning to "notice" each other. The girls began to flirt with boys who were completely clueless. It was causing awkwardness and it was causing dissension. I sent the boys out in their small group, and I spoke to the girls. I literally told them there would be no flirting when we were together. "We are a team. This is a safe place. We're family and family respects each other. No more flirting here at Wyldride." Their little mouths hung open and they all nodded at me. Believe it or not, that was the end of it. We had so created a team/family environment that they got it. I didn't have a problem after that.

The fruit of the team/family emphasis is kids today who are in their 20s and who love each other deeply. They support each other, connect with each other, and are there for each other. Nothing blesses my heart more than watching from afar on social media as they rally around one another. Even now, they are a team.

Hard questions: We will be a place where you can ask hard questions and wrestle with hard things. This is a safe place where you can begin to form your own opinions and ideas.

This was a tough one for me but it was also important. My

own journey in faith had often been dictated to me and I had found myself floundering in college realizing I believed things without knowing why. I wanted my kids to wrestle with the hard questions of faith in a safe place. The tough part was not giving them quick answers. Many a lesson was thrown out as they spent time as a group wrestling through their thoughts on new "provocative" movies, world events, games, music, or ideas. Probably the best thing I learned during those times was to ask more questions instead of give more answers. "What do you think about that?" and "Why do you think that?" Became my mantra.

We will have fun: We will laugh together and play together. This one seems trivial, but in reality, it is crucial. When you're teaching deep truth it's easy to get too serious. It's easy to get stuck in serious. I wanted my kids to understand how to have fun. How to laugh and play while still learning about God.

We played ridiculous games. I believe their favorite one is still Marshmallow Wars, which is basically throwing marshmallows at each other.

We had gingerbread house parties, ice cream sundae parties, and bonfires at Miss Mel's house.

We shared funny stories with each other. I would always share something personal and hilarious with them and they would share their stories with me.

We created an environment where we laughed, where we had fun, where we never took each other too seriously.

The fruit of that is kids who are quick to laugh and to find the humor in the situation instead of the negative.

Through the years and as my ministry has shifted, my list has shifted as well.

MY LIST TODAY

My list today looks something like this:

- God loves me and wants to be in a relationship with me.

- God created me on purpose for a purpose.

- I'm created in God's image. He made no mistakes on me.

- Even when I don't understand I can trust God.
- With God's help I can do hard things and love hard people.

These are my core beliefs that I drive home to kids. Woven throughout is the truth that having a relationship with Jesus means listening for Him. And it is always a given that we will have fun. We laugh hard and often. And while the Bible isn't listed, it has an intrinsic value. All five of these things are driven home by diving into God's story.

These are broad-based while being specific. I do that on purpose. I want to sit and park on the areas I feel led to park on. No matter what, I dig deep into these five things. I so firmly believe that kids need to know God loves them and desires to know them. I believe that kids need to know that they bear value. I believe kids need to understand that they can trust God. And I believe that following up those beliefs means putting our faith into action by loving hard people and doing hard things. The progression is purposeful. The progression is discipleship.

At the base of each of these things is my desire to give kids tools to do life in this world. This isn't about just giving them nice ideas or easy tools, this is about giving them solid truth that can change their lives. It takes the world into account while not diminishing the power of God.

We have little time with our kids. The more intentional and purposeful we can be, the better. God is a purposeful and intentional God. Discipling world changers means reiterating deep truths over and over and over again. And then doing it some more. Discipling world changers means giving our kids meat instead of milk, swords instead of marshmallows, and reality instead of fantasy. It means training them up today with a view of their tomorrow.

Hey Reader: What would your list be? Parent? Ministry leader? Ministry team? What is your list? I don't claim to have a perfect list, just one forged through my own experience and Holy Spirit heart-tugging. Without controlling your list will you ask these questions of your list?

1. Does it point kids to the heart of Jesus or to a certain behavior?
2. Will the truths bear up when the world gets loud and they feel all alone?
3. Does it give our kids tools to walk through the world they are growing up in?
4. Does your list focus on Jesus first or the world first?
5. Is your list aimed toward transformation or information?

CHAPTER SIXTEEN

A Safe Place to Wrestle

I SPEND A LOT OF MY TIME VISITING CHURCHES. Whether I'm a guest speaker, consultant, or just visiting because I'm in the area, I'm in a lot of churches. I have certain churches that I love. Not necessarily a specific church but a specific kind of church. I love the messy ones. Know what I mean? I love the churches that are a little bit of a hot mess. I like it when things aren't perfect.

My favorite services are a little loud. Kids make noise, adults talk to each other, and occasionally someone wanders up on stage who is not supposed to be on stage. My favorite church people are those who have lived a little life. They've come through deep waters, and it shows on them. They're in recovery, coming out of dysfunction, and every day is a battle. I find Jesus in those churches with those type of people.

The American church has strove for perfection for far too long. We've wandered away from the very heart of who Jesus is. He never once hung around with the perfect, in fact He waded into the messy and made His home there with them. In the Gospels, Jesus reminds people that it's not the healthy who need a doctor, but the sick (Mark 2:17, Luke 5:31). He reminds them that He came for the sinners, not the righteous. The very heart of Jesus was for the broken and the needy. I think He would delight in the churches that are filled with people who openly don't have it all together.

When we strive for perfection or put perfection on a pedestal, it speaks loudly to our kids. It gives them an ideal of what the Christian life should look like. It's completely unattainable because we all know that under the facade of perfection is raging imperfection.

For too long there has been an unwritten rule in many churches and Christian families that you have to have yourself somewhat together to do life well. And not just to attend the church, but to approach God. That message is not only wrong, it's unbiblical. When we do church or life that way, we send the message that if you have questions or you have issues you need to keep on moving and come back when you figure it out. I think that message must grieve the heart of the Father.

Discipling world changers is tied up in what we've been talking about: authenticity and reality. They need to know that loving Jesus doesn't mean you have to have it all figured out or that everything works perfectly. They need to see a little mess.

BIG QUESTIONS

Kids today have deep questions about God. Deep questions. Even if kids have never heard about God, they have questions about Him. The beauty of the God we serve is that we were created to be in relationship with Him. We will always hunger for Him, whether we know there is a "Him" or not. I talk to kids all the time who have no concept of God and yet they have questions about Him. Questions about His character, His abilities, and even His food choices. They are aching to know more about Him and very few of these little ones have a place where they are safe to ask their questions. We must provide a safe place for world changers to ask and wrestle with their big questions.

There are several reasons we as adults get nervous when kids start asking questions.

1. We're afraid we won't know the answer.

Let's be honest. Kids ask hard questions! They can be downright terrifying. We've all been there. A kid asks a question we don't know the answer to, and we freeze. I had a kid ask me how God murdered everyone with the flood when He couldn't sin. I have never prayed more fervently for the Second Coming as I did while he stared at me, unblinking, waiting for an answer.

2. We don't have the time.

We're busy people. If you're a parent, you're running in a hundred different directions and being pulled everywhere at once. You want to give your kids and their questions attention, but your phone is sending notifications and you're already late. If you're a teacher, you have precious few moments with kids and the pull of your lesson plan is strong.

3. We don't think it matters.

I'll say this as kindly as I can, but kids ask weird questions. It's easy to think that many of their questions don't matter. "Does God eat pizza?" "Who is God married to?" "Why are my boogers green?" In the midst of the busy we can tend to shrug off their questions thinking they don't matter much in the grand scheme of their lives.

A LESSON LEARNED

I learned a very important lesson between authoring *Missing* and authoring this book. I used to think I needed to have the answers. I was wrong. In fact, I have now learned that it is less about me knowing the answers and more about me giving permission for questions to be asked.

A number of years ago I was leading a retreat for a group of kids near Seattle. All of these kids came out of the womb smarter than I will ever be. Their parents were all high-level executives. It showed in the kids. They were smart, super smart. They were also still just kids like every other kid I've ever met. They had big questions, they were a little messy, and they were eager to learn. They were awesome.

During the retreat I allowed time for questions. I stood up in front of them, facilitating discussion and answering the questions as they came. They would ask questions and I would ask the group to contribute to the answer. One of the older boys raised his hand in the back and when I called on him everything changed.

"Miss Mel, how do you think the overall creation theory fits in with quantum mechanics?"

I am not often speechless, but I was completely flabbergasted. I desperately wanted to ask Siri for help but that was not an option with every eye in the room trained on me. He looked at me, I looked at him and out of sheer desperation I said, "I would really like to know what you think. Why don't you tell me about your thoughts on that subject?"

Sheer desperation people. There was nothing about that answer that was well thought out or strategic. I had absolutely no idea what quantum mechanics was, and I didn't have a hope of answering his question. I didn't want to lose face and admit to a tall eleven-year-old that I didn't know the answer to his question.

God in his graciousness allowed my completely lame answer to teach me an important lesson. The minute I asked the boy what he thought he let out a relieved breath and started to tell me exactly what he thought about quantum mechanics and the "creation theory." My discomfort went completely away as I stood there listening to him answer his own question. In that moment I realized that he hadn't been looking for an answer, he'd been looking for permission. That moment changed how I would do ministry with kids from that point on.

Let me say here that I wasn't purposely trying to elevate myself as some sort of genie with all the answers. I simply wanted kids to know it was okay to ask hard questions. I wanted to create space for them. However, by trying to answer their questions I was missing the point. They didn't necessarily need my answers, they needed me to give them space to wrestle with their hard questions. They needed to know it was okay to have hard questions.

Most kids who are asking tough questions have already thought them through. They already have an idea of what they think. It's our job to allow them to sigh in relief and be okay with their process of figuring it out.

If I'm making a disciple of me then kids need to come to me to get their answers. If I'm making a disciple of Christ, I help facilitate a safe place where they can take their tough questions to Jesus and wrestle with the answers.

BE QUIET MORE OFTEN

This is not to say that we're never supposed to answer kids's questions. There is a time and a place for that. We don't want to frustrate them. Neither do we want to put ourselves into a role that we were never meant to have. I want to suggest caution in this area. We don't need to have all of the answers. We don't need to have it all figured out. We don't need to resolve everything for them. I believe discipling world changers means we're quiet a little more often as we allow them to wrestle through the stirring God has placed in them. It's a beautiful, messy, not clearly defined dance.

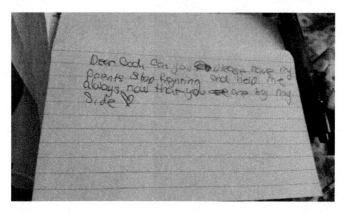

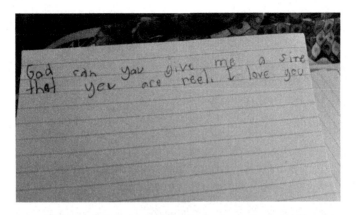

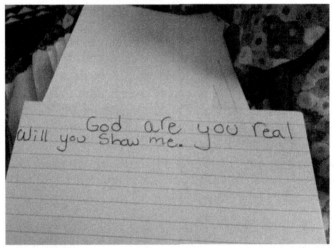

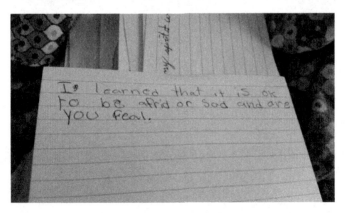

Hey Reader: Do some reflecting.

1. How can you create a safe place for the kids in your care?
2. How can you be quiet more often and leave room for God to do His work?
3. Spend some time praying and asking God to remind you that you don't need to know it all.

CHAPTER SEVENTEEN

Practical Examples

THIS CHAPTER IS ALL ABOUT PRACTICALITY. IT'S EASY to talk about theory in a book. I'm all about spurring you on to think for yourself. I also know what it's like to sit there thinking, "I got nothing!" With a sense of graciousness and understanding I want to give you some practical ideas for helping kids grasp Jesus as we disciple them toward being world changers. These are in no particular order, and there are certainly more to share. The idea is to give you some practical ideas. Use, tweak, and rearrange as needed.

He sees you. He knows you. He loves you. You decide.

I started this phrasing with kids a number of years ago. Kids do really well with repetitive phrasing and I wanted to give them some "meat" that would stick with them long after they left camp. This can easily be translated to a church program or with your kids at home. With kids third grade and under I do actions with it. He sees you (point to eyes), He knows you (point to head), He loves you (crisscross arms in front), you decide (say this loudly while pointing out with both fingers).

Encompassed in this phrase are four things I want to stick with kids:

Jesus sees you. He is always with you. He is always present in your life, and He sees you.

He knows you. Before you were born He knew you. He knows every little part about who you are. He knows what you think and what you feel. He knows your story.

He loves you. Jesus loves you. Completely, totally, forever. You can walk the progression of the phrase with kids. "God sees you. He knows all about you, and He loves you. Nothing you do can take that love away. He knows all about you and loves you."

You decide. This is where the rubber meets the road in this phrase. Kids know what they know but now they have to make a decision based on that knowledge. I often ask them, "What are you going to do with Jesus?" They decide. It's their choice. The facts are that He sees them, knows them, and loves them. The "Now what?" is up to them.

Scriptural Truth:

> **He sees you and knows you.** Psalm 139:13-16 NLT says, *"You made all the delicate, inner parts of my body and knit me together in my mother's womb. Thank you for making me so wonderfully complex! Your workmanship is marvelous— how well I know it. You watched me as I was being formed in utter seclusion, as I was woven together in the dark of the womb. You saw me before I was born. Every day of my life was recorded in your book. Every moment was laid out before a single day had passed."*

> **He loves you.** Ephesians 3:17-19 NLT says, *"Then Christ will make his home in your hearts as you trust in him. Your roots will grow down into God's love and keep you strong. And may you have the power to understand, as all God's people should, how wide, how long, how high, and how deep his love is. May you experience the love of Christ, though it is too*

great to understand fully. Then you will be made complete with all the fullness of life and power that comes from God."

This phrase can also easily be changed to make it personal. He sees me, He knows me, He loves me. I decide. It should be mentioned here that I would never teach all four of these things in one sitting. I'll teach them the phrase at the beginning of the week, and we'll repeat it all through the week while I unpack it. It's a simple way for kids to remember the character of who God is and that a relationship with Him is two-sided.

WE DON'T KNOW THEIR STORY

I covered Pineapple People in depth in *Missing*, but I want to touch on it here again and add a little something to it. Pineapple People is by far the most powerful lesson I teach to kids. Ever. I hear the most feedback from kids on this. Beyond that, this is the most powerful lesson I teach to adults. Ever.

Pineapple People are hurt people who hurt people. They're people who are mean to other people. They might be the bullies in the school, the kid who hits everyone, or the kid who always makes other people cry. They might be the parent who abuses, the older brother who yells, or the teacher who makes hurtful remarks.

Very few people like them. In a world that screams at us to look out for ourselves, Pineapple People are almost always misunderstood. They're pushed away, alienated, scoffed at, and hurt back. Our world says that's okay to do and it even says they're getting what they deserve. However, if we have decided to start a relationship with Jesus, we are called to live differently than the world tells us. We're called to love.

Luke 6:27-31 NLT says, *"But to you who are willing to listen, I say, love your enemies! Do good to those who hate you. Bless those who curse you. Pray for those who hurt you. If someone slaps you on one cheek, offer the other cheek also. If someone demands your coat, offer your shirt also. Give to anyone who asks and when things are taken away from you, don't try to get them back. Do to others as you would like them to do to you."*

The idea of love is all well and good until you're a kid and you're being bullied or made fun of or abused. The key phrase I use when explaining Pineapple People is, "We don't know their story."

I will always share a story about a Pineapple Person with kids. For example, suddenly the girl who was mean to me and I didn't like became a person I had compassion for and prayed for when I found out she didn't feel safe at home. The key for kids is opening their minds to the reality that people hurt people because they've been hurt. I have yet to see compassion lived out in any adult like it is in a child. Once they understand the hurt part, even an unpleasant person's pain breaks their hearts. I've had sixth grade girls weeping in repentance over how they treated a classmate and boys pouring their hearts out to Jesus because they've hurt others.

The other side to Pineapple People is the personal side. The idea is that you're likely addressing Pineapple People in your audience. They're kids who have been hurt so they're hurting others. I always explain that it's a cycle that goes on and on until someone says "stop" and decides to ask Jesus for help so they stop hurting other people. Again, I could go on and on with the stories of kids who have made the decision to stop the cycle.

Pineapple People are hurt people who hurt people. We don't know their story, but God does. We're called to show them love, to pray for them, and to have compassion for them.

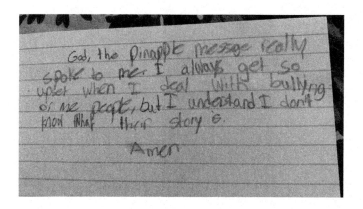

God, the pineapple message really spoke to me. I always get so upset when I deal with bullying or mean people, but I understand I don't know what their story is.
Amen

Lord help me not be a person that hurts others because someone hurt me. I don't wanna do that anymore.
—S

God You know Marquel. You love him. Help me be nice to him. I'm sure he has a hard story. I might be a pineapple person.
—M.

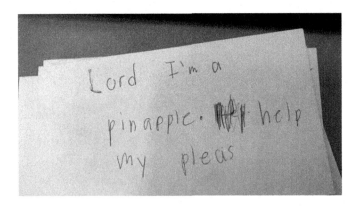

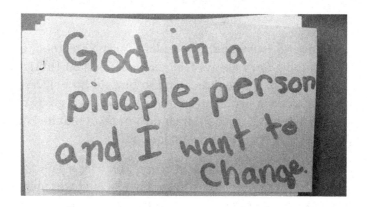

"TELL MY STORY"

Many years ago, as I was preparing for my first ever camp speaking engagement, I went away on retreat to prepare. I was at a cute little cabin somewhere in the middle of Iowa seeking God's heart. I kept asking God to give me certain gifts. The gifts I was asking for were based on what I had seen done by other people. "Lord, please give me the gift of puppets. Even though they scare me a little."

When that didn't seem to work I prayed for the gift of magic. That too was a no-go. I prayed for the ability to do science experiments. Nothing. I was scouring YouTube and Google for object lessons when God finally broke through to me. "Just tell My story" was His word to me. The phrase "tell my story" began resonating in my heart. I began to doodle it in my notebook and I suddenly realized God's story was enough.

I didn't need to jazz it up. I just needed to use my gifts and abilities and tell His story. That is exactly what I do. I'm a storyteller, it's who God designed me to be. So I tell kids God's story. The story layouts I share next are meant to be layered with what I shared earlier in this book. I permeate God's story with who God is and how that matters to kids. I insert core beliefs that I want to sink deep into kids's hearts. Here are some practical ideas for you:

Joseph

1. Choose to trust God. God's plans for me are good, even though they don't always feel good. Genesis 50:19-21. Tell the ending first. Joseph is going to be sold into slavery by his brothers. He's going to be put in prison. He's going to be scared, lonely, and sad. In the midst of all of that he knows that God is in control and God is good.

Personal: Your life might be scary. You might feel lonely and sad a lot of the time. You are loved. God loves you and His plans for you are good, even though they don't always feel good. It's up to you to choose to trust that God is with you, even when it doesn't feel like it.

Note: This is a great place for the salvation message.

2. Choose to notice God. Genesis 39:2 NLT. God was with Joseph. In verse 5 the Lord blesses Potiphar's household for Joseph. In verse 21 the Lord was with Joseph in prison, and "showed him his unfailing love."

Personal: God is always with you. He is there, but you have to choose to notice Him. Even when life seems crazy hard, God doesn't leave you.

Note: Don't be afraid of Potiphar's wife. I tell kids that she thought Joseph was good-looking. She wanted to kiss Joseph, so Joseph got out of there. Be sure you don't skip important parts of the story just because you're uncomfortable or unsure.

3. Choose to be a good friend. Genesis 40:6. Joseph noticed his friends looked upset. His life was hard, but he chose to be good friend and not only think about himself.

Personal: It's easy to only think about ourselves when we're having a rough time. Good friends notice their friends and look out for their friends.

Note: The dreams aren't the important part of the chapter for this example. Focus on Joseph's choice to be selfless and show kindness, like a good friend.

4. Choose to live your life in a way that points to God. Genesis 41:16. Joseph makes it clear to Pharaoh that he cannot interpret dreams, only God can. In verse 28, he reiterates that it was God who revealed the message, not himself. Because Joseph continually points to God instead of himself, his choices affected the whole story and people began to notice God. In verse 38, Pharaoh points out that Joseph is obviously filled with the spirit of God.

Personal: When we choose to start a relationship with God, we choose to live our lives in a way that points to Him. It means we remember that He is with us and that He gives us our gifts and talents. When we point to God, others begin to see Him and want to know more about Him.

Note: Don't get bogged down in the dreams. Focus on Joseph's part in the story and how his life is a testimony.

5. Choose your attitude. Genesis 42-44. This is by far one of the most suspenseful parts of this story. Kids loves it. Walk them through Joseph's responses. At no point does he choose bitterness, or choose to be unkind, or choose to hide, or choose to be spiteful. He chooses his attitude in every moment.

Personal: We don't get to always choose what happens to us but we do get to choose how we respond. Our attitude matters. The attitude we choose helps change the story.

Note: Walk your kids through this carefully. They can keep reading themselves but let the suspense remain.

6. Choose to love and forgive Pineapple People. Genesis 45, Genesis 50. We know a little about of Joseph's brothers's stories. They weren't the favorite sons. They felt jealous and left out and their feelings led them to make poor choices. They were Pineapple People. Joseph showed incredible compassion and love to them. He understood that God was in control and he told them not to be afraid.

Personal: This life is hard. You will get hurt, you will meet Pineapple People, but how you respond matters. Choosing to show love and forgiveness points your Pineapple People right to Jesus.

Note: Feel this story with the kids. It's an incredible story of grace, perspective, forgiveness, and God's sovereignty. Let it affect you as you share it with kids.

Daniel

1. Choose what to do with Jesus. Walk through the salvation message. The consequence of sin is death. Jesus provided a way out. Life with Jesus is hard but it's the best decision you'll ever make. Yet it is still your decision. He wants a relationship with you but you decide what to do with Jesus. Daniel 1:1-7. Give a teaser for Daniel. He is going to be kidnapped and never reunited with his family but he is going to change history. He knows God and follows God and because of that his story is amazing.

Personal: You decide what you do with Jesus. He sees you, He knows you, He loves you. You decide. Life is hard. Life with Jesus isn't easy but you are never alone. What will you do with Jesus?

2. Choose to follow God even when it's hard. Daniel 1. Daniel and his friends were kidnapped and forced to serve a king they didn't know. They had a choice, to either follow God or turn away from Him. They chose to follow Him and do what they knew was right even though it was hard.

Personal: It is often not easy to follow God. It's hard to feel different than other people. It's a choice we make to follow

God even when it's hard. He sees us, He knows us, He loves us. We decide.

3. Choose to trust. Your choices always affect you and everyone around you. Daniel 3. Shadrach, Meshach, and Abednego choose to trust God. In verses 16-18, they make it clear that they trust Him completely and that they are going to follow Him. They chose to trust and their choice changed the heart of a king. In verse 28, King Nebuchadnezzar starts praising God because He is so powerful. Their choices pointed others to God.

Personal: Choosing to trust means opening our hands up and surrendering to God. If we trust Him, He is big enough for our fears, our worries, our hopes, and our dreams. He is trustworthy but you decide what to do with Him.

4. Choose your attitude. Daniel's story starts with him being kidnapped and it doesn't end with him being back home. In fact, he never goes back home. Instead, he adopts a new country and a new king and a new way of life. He may not have liked his circumstances or even have been in control of what happened to him but he could choose his attitude. In Daniel 6 his life is threatened and he still chooses his attitude and chooses to live his life in a way that pointed to God.

Personal: We aren't in control of what happens to us, but we are in control of how we respond to it. I can guarantee Daniel was not thrilled to be thrown into a pit of lions and yet his attitude made a huge difference in the story. He chose to follow God, he chose to be who he was, he chose to trust, and he chose his attitude. As a result, King Darius had a new understanding of who God is. It changed the whole story.

Note: Enter into this story. It's incredible! Spend some time imagining what it would be like to be surrounded by lions. What would it be like to know what was coming your way but still choosing to trust God? What was it like to be King Darius? Kids love this story. Keep it fresh and enter into it.

Other options:

5. Choose to love and forgive. The accumulation of Daniel growing where he was planted and not choosing bitterness.

6. Choose to live your life in a way that points to God. Go back through and highlight the moments where Daniel and the other guys lived their lives uprightly and it changed the lives of the people around them.

David

1. Will you choose to receive or deny the gift you've been given? 1 Samuel 16. In verse 2 Samuel was obedient even though he was afraid of Saul. In verse 11 he's obedient again even though he must have been tired after a long journey. David chose to serve Saul even though he was at risk. David accepted and followed the path God had laid out for him. He could have said no but he chose to receive the gift he was being given.

Personal: David was obedient and faithful. He most likely didn't always like the path that was laid out for him but he chose to keep going. Pull in Jeremiah 29:11. God's plans for him were good, although they won't always feel good. You've been offered a big gift from God. What will you do with it? It's your choice. God sees your heart (1 Samuel 16:7) and He wants to be in a relationship with you.

Note: One of the kids's favorite phrases is from 1 Samuel 16:2. Samuel is worried about going and Saul finding out. We say that God basically said, "Don't have a cow, take a cow," referring to the heifer Samuel is to take with him. The kids found that to be hilarious and repeated it ALL the time. The beauty is explaining that sometimes we don't always understand what God is doing or saying and yet He still has a plan. In Samuel's case, we see the heifer was part of his protection in verse 5.

This is a great place for the salvation message.

2. Will you choose to trust or be fearful? 1 Samuel 17. Walk through David and Goliath. David chooses to be obedient and courageous because he trusts God. Choice after choice he makes is significant. Our choices always affect us and the people around us. David trusts God and his choices flow out of that trust. In verses 45 and 47 he has the opportunity to point to himself but instead points out that it is God who has done great things.

Personal: What do you need to trust God with? This is a great place for you to share personally about a tough time you've gone through. God doesn't always make sense but He is trustworthy. It's our choice. What do you need to trust God with? Open your hands in surrender.

Note: This is my favorite story to tell! Get into it. Put yourself in David's place, in his brother's place, in the place of the friend who stays behind and watches David's sheep. Look at this through new eyes and bring kids along with you.

3. What kind of attitude will you choose? 1 Samuel 18. Walk through the attitudes Saul chose. Jealously, fear, and hate. In verses 28-29 we see that Saul begins to hate David. Jealously led to fear and fear led to hate. There is a ripple effect when we sin and we don't let God take over and help us.

Personal: Our attitudes matter. We can't control what happens to us but we can control how we respond. Compare and contrast David and Saul's attitudes. What attitude will you choose when life gets hard or doesn't go your way?

4. Will you choose to see God at work? 1 Samuel 19-20. Walk through these two chapters. God is always at work around us. We have to look for Him and acknowledge Him. David is running for his life and yet he is provided with a good friend in Jonathan. God is always present in both the hard and easy, the sadness and the joy. God never wastes our pain. He uses what is hard to teach us and help us understand Him more. Look for God everywhere.

Personal: God is there. Look for Him. Choose to trust He's there and choose to look for Him. Even when the journey is hard God provides blessings along the way. Jonathan was one of God's blessings. Where have you seen God blessing you? Where do you need to focus on the positive instead of the negative?

5. Will you choose to forgive or hate? 1 Samuel 24 and 26. Walk through the different times where David chooses not to kill Saul. Where he chooses to acknowledge that Saul's life has value even though he's hurt him deeply. Pineapple People. Hurt people hurt people but only we can stop the cycle.

Personal: We're called to live and look differently in this world. We're called to show love and grace and kindness and forgiveness to those who hurt us. If we love Jesus we love people differently. We do things the world thinks is strange. We care when people are hurting. Instead of being angry, we're compassionate and we forgive. Who do you need to forgive today? Who is your pineapple person that you feel God may be asking you to show love and forgiveness to? Who do you need to start praying for instead of being angry at?

Hey Reader:

1. What Bible characters came to mind for you to possibly tell the story of?
2. What points stood out to you? Why?
3. What main points would you add?

CHAPTER EIGHTEEN

World Changers

I CAN THINK OF NO BETTER WAY TO CLOSE THIS BOOK than to tell you the stories of some world changers. Real life people who are changing the world. Real life people who have encountered God and have been changed forever. Real life people who are walking forward in the midst of this crazy hard world we live in.

Clavie

It was the second day of camp. I was in the middle of an intense game of Nine Square.

I should mention that as a young children's pastor some of my team was kind enough to let me know I was a little too competitive to play games with children. I always play to win, and I tend to be verbal. I think it was after a couple of my team members found me yelling at my foosball "men" to "get your act together and beat these guys!" that they had an intervention with me. I'd like to think I've matured since then. In the last few years I have cautiously inserted myself into a few kid games while lecturing myself that "it's just a game and you don't have to win."

All that to say I was playing Nine Square and beating the socks off of the group of fifth and sixth graders that had gathered to play. I'm not exactly sure what happened but one moment I was hitting the ball and the next minute I collided with a small blond-haired boy. He landed on the ground as I hit the winning shot. He rolled around the ground grabbing his shoulder yelling, "My clavicle, I broke my clavicle!"

While not exactly a Nine Square star, this little guy could easily have a spot on the stage at some point in his life. His dramatic effects were real although his clavicle was fine. I did the age-old dance of showing sympathy while assessing his "injuries" and finally making him laugh. I couldn't get over the fact that he had been hollering about his clavicle. Pretty soon the whole group was laughing together with him about his dramatic clavicle declaration. After a little ice application, he joined back in the game. From that point on I referred to him as "Clavie" and coincidentally the whole camp began to call him that.

Clavie and I formed a bond. He and I connected often throughout the week. He was a fun-loving kid who had a quick smile and the ability to laugh at himself. I loved him.

The morning chapel of our last day of camp is when the kids share what God taught them that week. They line up and I interview them about what God showed them throughout the week at camp. It's one of my favorite parts of the week. I always preface the focus very clearly to minimize the kids who get up to share a bathroom or snoring story just for a laugh. The kids who get up almost always have something very real to share.

I was working through the line of kids when I saw Clavie in line. As he moved through the line, I smiled at him. When it was his time to speak the whole camp was cheering for him, "Clavie! Clavie! Clavie!" He was enjoying every minute of it and fist-pumping his way around the stage. He had quickly become the most popular kid at camp. Miss Mel had given him a nickname, he was hilarious, and everyone liked him.

In all honesty, I expected very little from his sharing. He was a ham, and I fully expected him to be shallow. He had stolen a part of my heart, so I let him rally the crowd for a minute before I asked him what God had taught him. To my utter shock he grew incredibly serious and the whole camp settled down and stared at him. His eyes got misty as he firmly announced, "God spoke to me and told me I'm going to be a missionary in Haiti. I was doing my devotions a couple days ago and that's what God told me so that's what I'm going to do."

What happened next still brings tears to my eyes. Clavie announced his calling to a still and sacred room full of kids. As one they gasped and started cheering and applauding for him. They were not the cheers of a rowdy group looking for a way to go crazy. They were the cheers of affirmation and confirmation from his peers. It was holy and nearly brought me to my knees. With tears in my eyes I affirmed Clavie and then we prayed over him. And when I say prayed, I mean all 200 kids reached out their hands and prayed over Clavie. As a camp we commissioned him.

In the summer of 2022, a camp counselor with blond curly hair walked up to me at camp. "Do you remember me?"

"CLAVIE!"

It was him. That same Clavie was now a camp counselor at the same camp where God had met him so powerfully. I asked him if he remembered his commission and he interrupted me to say, "Oh I remember. I've never forgotten."

Mohawk Kid

I noticed him the very first day at camp. He sat to my right as I spoke to the kids. He sat alone and was in a fairly isolated spot on the floor. As a seasoned camp speaker, I've learned to ignore a lot of things when I'm speaking. This little guy with a mohawk seemed to hear his own music. While I was speaking, he would slowly rotate his arms around his head as if conducting his own music. Every now and then he would twitch. He was not disruptive, but he was noticed, by me.

I learned a long time ago that kids rarely look like they are listening and yet most often they are listening. The little guy in my audience gave absolutely no indication that he was listening let alone comprehending anything I was saying. I've also learned not to judge a person's story by their behavior. I knew he had a story and I wondered ...

His sister had shared her story with me earlier in the week.

"I started doing Marijuana with my cousins when I was 7. On the Res everyone did drugs, it's different there. I would deliver drugs to my aunt but I didn't know the package was drugs. I just thought she wanted to see me, but no. I've been in about 200 foster homes. The parent I'm closest to is my dad but now he's in prison for life and doesn't want me. My mom is in prison too and she doesn't want me either. At age 10 I started doing hardcore drugs. I didn't know it wasn't ok. I didn't know it could harm you. Then I started going to church and was told God loved me no matter what and my back story didn't change God's love. I was sent here to camp as a punishment and it worked (I hate that my foster parents were right!). I started a relationship with Jesus last night. I feel happy, I feel different. I want to do good things now."

This 12 year old broke me as she told me her story this morning. I mean broke me. Puddle on the floor. Her favorite word is Emmanuel, "because it means God's always with me. Always."

I grabbed this little one's face, looked her in the eye and blessed her. Not because it was comfortable or easy but because God told me to do it. "I bless you for your bravery. I bless you for sharing your story. May you know deep in your soul that you are loved and never alone. May you never forget that God has redeemed you and called you by name. I bless you as you begin to see God weave beauty out of your messy story.

You are worthwhile and you are loved." And then she went inside and Miss Mel had a very messy breakdown.

Through the course of her sharing her story I put together that her little brother was also at camp. Her brother was my little mohawk kid. She rushed to assure me, "He's had it a lot easier than me. He's only nine and he's only been in two foster homes." She told me he had recently been diagnosed with autism. Before she shared some of her story with the camp the next morning, I asked her if her brother would be okay with her sharing. She told me he wouldn't understand any of it.

I kept my eye on that little mohawk kid. I learned his name and watched him interact (or not interact) with other kids. There was no question he had some difficulties. His speech seemed to be severely limited. I actually never heard him talk. I knew that although his sister thought he had had it easier, he had been significantly affected by his home life and present abandonment. Of course, my heart broke.

Toward the end of camp, he came up to me while we were swimming and we "talked" briefly. He floated in his life jacket and just beamed at me. He seemed content to just be near me. Of course, he stole my heart.

On the last day of camp, kids shared what God had taught them that week. I had a long line of kids up front sharing. I did a double-take when Little Mohawk was at the end of the line. I went through twenty kids and in the back of my head I wondered how I was going to handle him. I knew he couldn't talk and I wasn't sure why he was in line. He was the last kid to go and I treated him the same way I had every other kid. I said his name and asked him, "What's God been teaching you this week?" I held my breath as he smiled at me and his mouth struggled to form words. It seemed the whole camp held their breath because there was silence until he burst out with the word, "Love!"

It wasn't entirely clear but everyone could identify the word. I repeated "love" and he smiled and bobbed his head at me. Without prompting the entire group did a little gasp and started cheering and clapping for him. He smiled until I thought his face would break.

As he walked off stage, I took a minute to compose myself.

When I turned back around, he had grabbed his stuff and moved to sit in the very middle of the room surrounded by kids. And he kept smiling.

I had to leave camp right after that last chapel. Kids were high-fiving and hugging me goodbye. Little Mohawk came up to me still smiling. I opened my arms, and he dove in and gave me a huge hug. I hugged him back and held my tears.

Liz

I'm not entirely sure when I met Liz, as I don't have a memory of our first meeting. All I know is she was suddenly in my world. I was fifteen and her midweek games leader at our church. She was ten and one of "those" kids. I remember taking her out of a game because she was doing something naughty. When she was fourteen, she was in my summer high school girls Bible study. When she was fifteen, she was on a visit at Crown College where I was a student and I was able to pray with her to start a relationship with Jesus. When she was nineteen, she moved to Idaho and became my summer children's ministry intern. What originally was a three-month internship turned into a three-year experience.

Liz grew up in dysfunction. It was all she knew. When she came to live with me it was a completely new way of doing life for her. Boundaries, expectations, social graces, and more were expected in my home. She rose to the occasion over and over again, although it wasn't easy. I knew God had His hand on her. I also saw the old way of doing things pulling frantically at her. More than one night was spent on my knees doing battle in prayer for her.

Liz began to make radical changes and chose to walk forward into the light. God in His grace began to write a new story for her. Our relationship ebbed out of a mother/daughter type relationship into a friendship. She got her own place and spread her wings. When I contracted a debilitating disease, Liz stepped in and ran my children's ministry. When I had reconstructive knee surgery she moved back in to take care of me.

We both moved away from Idaho. She went to college in Georgia, and I became a missionary in Austria. We encouraged each other and spurred each other on from afar. I was at her college graduation. I moved her to Wisconsin. She has spent every Christmas as an adult with my family. She's *become* family.

Liz is a next generation pastor today. She leads with confidence. She thinks outside of the box and daily points people to Jesus. She's not perfect but she keeps walking forward. I know if I gave her space in this book, she would write about the impact I've had on her. Instead, I see the impact she's had on me. Discipleship is like that. It's iron sharpening iron. It's learning from each other. It's doing life together for the long haul. Liz is a world-changer.

Allie (told in her own words)

After youth group one night, some of us middle school girls decided it would be neat to have a Bible study at school. The next morning, I stopped in to talk with our principal about if that was a possibility. He said that our music teacher had talked to him the week before about starting a Bible study for middle school girls, but he told her that she couldn't lead it or organize it. It would have to be a student lead study and group. He said I could talk to her and get something going.

We had our first study the next Monday after school. We knew we had track practice after school as well, so we talked to the track coach, and asked if we could come to track late and still get our workout in. He said that would be fine. We had 12th, 7th and 8th graders come to the first meeting. After Bible study, we walked to track practice, checked in with the coach to get our running assignment, and finished our workout. After we were finished, we checked in with the coach again to see if there was anything else we should do, and he told us no, that we were good to go. We were all so excited about everything that had happened. We went to have pizza together for supper.

The next day we had a track meet. Sometime between the time we left the track on Monday (when everything was fine) and the time that we were loading the bus to go to the track meet on Tuesday, SOMETHING HAPPENED! When we were on our way to the track meet, the coach stood up on the bus and said that if you were one of the girls who missed part of practice yesterday, that you had to run extra today before the track meet or you couldn't participate. He told us that our first priority had to be track, and then asked us, "What is your first priority?"

Lots of the girls said track, and I said, "God!"

He said, "No, if you are on the team, track is your first priority." He told us again that if we wanted to participate we had to make track our first priority and run the extra laps. I told him I was NOT going to run the extra laps, and if that meant I couldn't participate, I wouldn't participate in the track meet. Eight of the other girls who went to the Bible study joined me in standing up in the fact that GOD is our first priority. They didn't participate in the track meet either. It wasn't about running the two extra laps—it was about wanting the coach, and the other people on the team to know that track is important, but it isn't the most important thing to me. While we were at the track meet, I had the mother of one of the other girls on our team come up to me and say, "You are a leader. If you would have run and participated, all those other girls would have too." I felt like I was a leader, because that night after the track meet I had two girls want to know about Jesus. To me, if I could help two girls know Jesus that is way more important than a track meet.

Josh

I was fresh out of college when I met Joshua. He was a precocious nine-year-old that barely reached my elbow. I was candidating for the position of Children's Pastor at a church in Orlando, Florida. The church decided it would be a fun activity to take the candidate on a river tubing experience. The pastor and his family brought Joshua along to ride in the car with me. It was a not-so-subtle way of seeing how I interacted with kids.

Tubing on a river in Florida meant some truly terrifying dangers that this Midwestern girl had no concept of. Alligators, snakes, spiders, etc. Our guide cautioned us to stay on our tubes at all times. I set off with the group and my ever-present shadow, Josh, bouncing on his tube next to me. About an hour into the tour Joshua fell off his tube. He was yelling for help and waving his arms. Let me pause here to say, the river was moving at the speed of about half a mile every hour and was about two feet deep. Joshua yelled for help and my tube was moving away from him. In a split-second, I weighed all the pros and cons and decided to leave him. Safety first. I left the kid! I yelled for him to stand up and relax. Another person was already coming up to rescue him. He was fine. Later that day we were back in the pastor's van and the pastor asked Josh what he thought of "Miss Melissa." Josh loudly declared, "She tried to drown me!" My mouth hung open in shock and then we all started laughing. That was the moment that kids stole my heart forever.

Through my time at that church as his children's pastor, Joshua was the shadow that never left me. He always had a story, an encouraging word, and a comment about my hair. He was that kind of kid. When he decided to be baptized, I was the pastor he wanted to baptize him. I was beyond honored to be his pastor. When it came time for me to move on nobody took it harder than Josh. He was heartbroken.

What should have been a natural moment for separation was anything but. Josh and I were linked. He called me regularly. As a young teen he was saving money to come visit me. He called me to talk about his dog, his family, his sadness, his dreams, and more. I think he was twelve when I told myself, "I'm going to be at that kid's wedding." I knew when he was thirteen that he would work with students someday.

I watched my sweet Josh grow into a man. Over the years, there were very few big moments in his life I wasn't a part of. When he knew he was called to ministry, he called me. When he met the girl of his dreams, he called me. When he asked his girl to marry him, he called me. Through the years I watched Josh grow in his relationship with Jesus and his ability to love people. He inspired me as he loved people out loud. He was actively in their lives. When he got married, I was there. I tried to sneak in the back, but he found me and seated me next to his parents in the front row. His mama grabbed my hand as I tried to sneak away and with tears in her eyes said, "You sit here. You are his spiritual mama. You sit here with me." We shared tissues and cried all the tears as he married his bride. I gave a toast at his reception and cried more tears.

Josh and his wife Kari miscarried two babies. I've grieved

with them both times. As their marriage has gone through trials and joys, I walk with them. Josh and Kari just welcomed their third baby and hardly a day goes by that I don't pray for them. Their very lives point people to Jesus. I'm so proud of them.

That's what discipleship looks like. It's that life-on-life, moment by moment stuff. It's the funny stories and the gut-wrenching stories. It's the hard conversations and the encouraging conversations. As I watch Josh and his wife love Jesus, I know they are world changers. They are tangible examples that discipleship is worth it. It reminds me that God is gracious, and it is so not about me. That I get to glimpse into His plans it is more than enough.

I could write a whole book of stories about world changers. They are out there. They are living for Jesus even though the world thinks they are weird. They have been discipled, are being discipled, and are changing the world. Much like our great men and women of faith from Hebrews 11, they might have a couple monumental moments here and there but most often they are choosing to obediently walk forward in faith. They are daily putting one foot in front of the other and choosing Jesus moment after moment.

What is even more exciting is the world changers that are being raised up even now. They're in your home, in your church, in your community, in your camp, in your school. God has equipped them to change the world. Now it's our honor and job to intentionally walk with them.

May my legacy, may our legacy, be the world changers that come behind us. May they love deeper, walk farther, and know more about radical change than we ever will.

End Notes

Chapter 1

Holy Bible: New Living Translation. (2004). Tyndale House Publishers.

Chapter 2

Holy Bible: New Living Translation. (2004). Tyndale House Publishers.

Chapter 3

Holy Bible: New Living Translation. (2004). Tyndale House Publishers.

Chapter 4

Holy Bible: New Living Translation. (2004). Tyndale House Publishers.

Powell, K., & Clark, C. (2011). *Sticky Faith: Everyday Ideas to Build Lasting Faith in Your Kids.* Zondervan.

When did Sunday schools start? (2008, August 28). Christian History | Learn the History of Christianity & the Church. https://www.christianitytoday.com/history/2008/august/ when-did-sunday-schools-start.html

Chapter 5

Holy Bible: New Living Translation. (2004). Tyndale House Publishers.

Chapter 8

Holy Bible: New Living Translation. (2004). Tyndale House Publishers.

Chapter 9

Blackaby, H., & King, C. V. (1990). *Experiencing God: Knowing and Doing the Will of God.* Lifeway Church Resources.

Holy Bible: New Living Translation. (2004). Tyndale House Publishers.

Chapter 11

Holy Bible: New Living Translation. (2004). Tyndale House Publishers.

Chapter 12

Holy Bible: New Living Translation. (2004). Tyndale House Publishers.

Chapter 17

Holy Bible: New Living Translation. (2004). Tyndale House Publishers.

Acknowledgments

WRITING A BOOK TAKES A VILLAGE … AND VILLAGES. Unlike my first book—where I took six weeks away to write—this one was forged over a year in stolen moments on airplanes, in hotel rooms, at my dining room table, in friends' houses, and in places from Washington to Puerto Rico to New York to Austria. I was given grace upon grace by so many people in my life.

To my neighbor girls, "the neighbs", who respected when I couldn't "come out and play" and willingly interrupted me when I could. You girls are my besties. You keep me grounded. You are always up for a dance party in my kitchen, and you bring light into my home every time you come over. I love you.

To Dan Wetzel who has never once stopped spurring me on, challenging me, and encouraging me to ground myself in scripture. Thank you, Dan, for being so consistently the face of Jesus in my life.

To Joshua. You were my first "kid." You never fail to give me a glimpse of Heaven as you allow me to journey alongside you and Kari. I love that I still get to be one of your pastors. I'm incredibly proud of you and how you continue to cling to Jesus and walk forward.

To Keith and Kathy Davis who help me sort through my "crazy" as often as I need it. You are always willing to listen, give advice, and keep me healthy. I'm so incredibly grateful for your presence in my life both as counselors and as friends.

To my sister and brother-in-law, Thylin and Reese. You never stop cheering me on, are always willing to talk deep about Jesus, and no matter how many times you hear me speak, you are always willing to come hang out and hear me again. I'm so proud of you. You have both shaped me and I'm so grateful for you.

To Liz. You push me and encourage me. You laugh with me (and at me). You continue to be one of my biggest cheerleaders. Thank you for seeing in me what I never could and calling it out in me. I'm so proud of you.

To you kids (young and old) who have given me permission to hear your story. I'm a better pastor, speaker, author, and person because of the imprint you have made on me.

To Chicken Nugget. You made me a parent (foster) and have taught me more about the heart of Jesus than anyone else ever has. Thanks for letting me borrow your markers for my writing weekend and for sending me silly videos. You are forever imprinted on my heart.

To my Honeybunny. I wrote this first draft while falling in love with you. Our love was so new, you didn't even make it in the acknowledgments yet. Then I rewrote this book after four years of marriage and in the midst of our foster care journey. You have always said "yes" and "go" and "I'm so proud of you." We are better together—exactly what we both prayed for. Thank you for seeing me for who I am, loving me for me, and cheering me on 110%. I'm so honored to do this messy, beautiful life alongside you.

Lastly, to Jesus. The Author of my story. The One who began the stirring in my soul that told me it was time to start writing again. I love serving You. Let's do this forever.

About the Author

MELISSA J. MACDONALD HAS DEDICATED OVER TWO decades to full-time ministry experience, with a profound commitment to serving ministry leaders and children on a global scale. Her journey includes a ten-year tenure supporting children's ministry leaders within a global denomination, participation in the Global Children's Forum, and an active role on the board of INCM (International Network of Children's Ministry). Alongside her speaking, writing, and coaching, Melissa has dedicated her life to walking alongside leaders and empowering children to encounter Jesus in a way that changes them forever.

Renowned for her captivating speaking style, Melissa effortlessly blends humor, profound truths, and real-life anecdotes to engage and inspire her audience.

Melissa and her Guatemalan-born husband, Luis, make their home in Iowa, where they actively participate in their community and serve as foster parents.

For more information, please visit
www.melissajmacdonald.com.